What pec

AEROSM

"Meet The Armstrongs! And climb onboard for their joyous ride into the Heart of Rock & Roll!"
—John Dossett, Tony-nominated actor

* * *

"Personal, and told with enthusiasm and verve, the stories reveal exactly why rock music has captured the imagination of millions for almost sixty years. Rock is the music of modern America and the Armstrong's book is a fun ride through one family's Rock & Roll Journey."
—Dr. Kenneth Bindas, author of S*wing, That Modern Sound: The Cultural Context of Swing Music in America* and many other historical publications

* * *

"I love the father-daughter team of Terry and Moira Armstrong! Strengthening their bond each year through the experience of Rock and Roll. Their stories show their love of music, family, friends and of course their hometown of Warren, Ohio in Northeast Ohio. *Aerosmith to ZZ Top: A Dad and Daughter's Rock and Roll Journey* shows they take full advantage of our local music scene, including trips to Dave Grohl Alley (Warren is Dave's birthplace), community favorite summer concert series River Rock at the Amp, and the many concerts they rocked out in at the historic Packard Music Hall. Enjoy riding along their many journeys!"
—Beth Kotwis Carmichael, Executive Director of Trumbull County (OH) Tourism

* * *

"Aerosmith to ZZ Top will make readers envious of Terry and Moira Armstrong's concert adventures...and their father-daughter relationship."

—Andy Gray, Entertainment Editor for the *Tribune Chronicle* and *The Vindicator*

* * *

"Ohio-based father and daughter Terry and Moira Armstrong open up their years-spanning (and well-traveled) treasure trove of concert memories to rock-and-roll fans. Through photos and stories, they chronicle shared experiences of attending generation-defying shows, ranging from Aerosmith to ZZ Top, with long and poetic passages written on Bruce Springsteen and the E Street Band and Joan Jett, whom the Armstrongs met backstage and the act they've seen the most—seven times. What could be a a list of concert reviews transforms into deeper stories on identity, loss, familial bonding, and the melding of two different generations, all seen through the lens—and power—of rock and roll. This wholesome family-friendly memoir is a must for anyone who has a passion for music and the kind of intimate storytelling only rock and roll can channel."

—Garin Pirnia, arts and culture writer for several publications as well as author of *Rebels and Underdogs: The Story of Ohio Rock and Roll* and *The Beer Cheese Book*

* * *

"This book is fun! Natural and conversational, I loved riding along for the many musical adventures of a father-daughter team who love music, life and each other. Great writing, great stories and a real lift!"

—Mary Beth Tinker, activist and free speech pioneer (Tinker v. Des Moines)

* * *

"*From Aerosmith to ZZ Top* is a must read for any music lover. As someone who developed a love for rock and roll because of my own dad, this father-daughter music memoir really resonated with me. Each chapter really make you feel like you're on tour, travelling from concert to concert with Terry and Moira."

—Capri Cararo, author of *United We Eat: 50 Great American Dishes To Bring Us All Together*, Executive in Residence at American University's School of Public Affairs, and former Minority Leader in the Ohio Senate

* * *

"A fun and interesting read full of Northeast Ohio Rock and Roll spirit! Moira and Terry share the soundtrack of their lives through excellent storytelling from a unique father-daughter perspective. In a world that desperately needs it, Moira and Terry's concert adventures serve as an important reminder of the powerful bond that music can create. This book will inspire you to share a song or two with your own loved ones."

—Aaron Stubbs, Diversity and Inclusion Trainer/Consultant and former student of Terry's at LaBrae High School

A DAD & DAUGHTER'S ROCK & ROLL JOURNEY

MOIRA ARMSTRONG
AND
TERRY ARMSTRONG

NOODLE SALAD PUBLISHING

WARREN, OH

NOODLE
SALAD
PUBLISHING
WARREN,OH

FROM AEROSMITH TO ZZ TOP:

A DAD & DAUGHTER'S ROCK AND ROLL JOURNEY

Color Paperback ISBN: 978-1-7365720-0-9
Color Hardcover ISBN: 978-1-7365720-1-6
Ebook ISBN: 978-1-7365720-2-3
Black & White Paperback ISBN: 978-1-7365720-3-0

First Noodle Salad Publishing edition • June 2021

This book is dedicated to two amazing women:
one that we know very well and one that we feel like we do.

First, to the memory of Jane Scott,
the world's first rock reporter.

Jane worked for the *Cleveland Plain Dealer* and blazed the trail for journalists for years to come with her notepad and a jar of peanut butter. Her bronze statue sat in the Rock and Roll Hall of Fame atrium for many years, reminding Moira that writing about rock can be a job—and can be a job for girls with big glasses.

Second, to the greatest wife and mom in the world,
Kimberly Armstrong.

She has been there with us every time she could be and always supported us when she could not go, even though she often thinks we are a bit crazy with some of our excursions...which we are. We are so lucky to have her in our lives. She rocks, too!

Left: Moira with statue honoring Rock journalist Jane Scott at the Rock and Roll Hall of Fame

Below: Kim with Moira

TABLE OF CONCERTS

OPENING ACT

Foreword

As I walked into work in the Summer of 2012, I didn't realize it was going to be a special day in my life. That day I would meet two future life-long friends while heading in to perform. I have made my living as an actor, working mainly in NYC On and Off-Broadway, and for the last 20 years primarily in musical theater. But I love Rock and Roll. I still remember hearing "The Happening" by the Supremes, over the PA system at a fast food restaurant in 1965, and feeling a jolt of electricity surge through my body. Soon thereafter I would discover The Beatles, and life would never be the same. In a few years I would spend the exorbitant sum of 56 dollars on a combination radio and cassette player (You could tape songs right off the radio!). My first purchased cassette? The Beatles' *Help*. I grew up on the Three Bs: Beatles, Bruce, and Bowie. With a healthy dose of Cat Stevens, Elton John, Jethro Tull, Philly Soul, Motown, and all things that are now considered Classic Rock. I still remember watching The Beatles perform "Hey Jude" on the Ed Sullivan show. It was a magical time.

In the play *Golden Boy* by Clifford Odets there is a line that strikes me as one of those absolute truths you occasionally hear or read. The lead character, Joe, is a boxer but also a skilled violinist. He says, "With music you're never alone when you're alone." Truer words were never spoken. The first time I heard Bruce Springsteen, on the album *Greeting from Asbury Park* in the summer of 1975, I knew I would never be alone again. Bruce spoke to my very soul, and still does. The day that *Born To Run* was released, I was a senior in high school and cut classes so I could go to Sears and buy it. I sped home and listened to it, reading along with the lyrics on the album. I will never forget the thrill of that moment. It's #1 on my Desert Island albums. I've since seen Bruce 11 times in concert. He is the Grand Prophet of the redemptive power of Rock and Roll.

I actually met him in 1988. I was waiting for a friend to arrive and see a show together. As I'm peering down 43rd St, a car turned off of 9th Ave and parked on the corner. Now I'm not a car guy (I drive a 2003 Honda Pilot that I will cry bitter tears over when it finally dies), but this car caught my attention. It was sleek and low and curvy and a shade of metallic green I had never seen before. A woman got out of the passenger seat and walked into a bodega. I thought to myself, "I know that woman." Then it hit me. It was Patti Scialfa. Which must mean that Bruce is in that car! An immediate battle waged in my brain over whether to be cool or go bother him. Fortunately, common sense won and I found myself in the street tapping on his window. He looked up from the cassette he was holding and rolled down the window. Manually. I said, "I just wanted to let you know that your songs have been real good friends to me over the years." Bruce replied, "Oh, thanks, man." I waved and walked away. Perfect.

Back to the Summer of 2012. As I approached my theater, (I was playing Joseph Pulitzer in *Newsies*), I noticed a father and his daughter. Now I get to the theater over an hour before showtime so it's unusual that there are any audience members waiting when I arrive. They asked for a picture and I was happy to oblige. The girl seemed very sweet and shy, but I could feel her excitement. She was wearing a funny t-shirt about the unpredictability of Cleveland weather. As her Dad took the picture he quipped, "This is the first time I've ever taken a picture of someone wearing a Steelers cap." I didn't let the comment bother me. After all he's had to live with The Drive, The Fumble, The Shot, and the Cubs. (Thank the Heavens for LeBron!) They were very nice, and eager to see the show. We talked for a few moments and then I said goodbye and went inside. As I sat in my dressing I kept thinking about the girl I'd just met. There was just something about her. So I went back outside and asked if they'd like to come backstage after the show.

And that was my introduction to the Armstrongs, Terry and his daughter Moira. She seemed thrilled to be standing on the stage after the performance and I introduced her to some of the other cast members. I later received a letter in the mail from Terry thanking me for the experience I'd given his daughter. As a parent I understood that. My son Jack is her age and I want nothing more than to fill his life with memorable moments. Terry told me they were coming back to see the show and I said we should have dinner afterwards. We did, and that was the beginning of an acquaintance that has turned into a friendship. We have met many times over the years (They will drive anywhere!), and have bonded over our numerous shared interests, none more than Rock and Roll! I have witnessed Moira's transformation from shy teenager to confident young adult, who I know is going to conquer the world! (Let's all start that letter writing campaign to the R&R Hall of Fame about getting her an Internship!) The last time I saw them, we talked so long that we closed the restaurant. I eagerly look forward to the time we can rendezvous again. And to finally meeting Kim!

I love this book. It's fun and funny, informative (The Tallest Man On Earth? Who knew!), oftentimes quite poignant, and filled with great stories. And it is so absolutely *them*. They are what was once termed "Salt of the Earth" type people. You can't help seeing the decency, kindness, and living-life-to-the-fullest/sense-of-fun they exude. It's no wonder so many people have gone out of their way to give them "beyond my wildest dreams" moments. Good things happen to good people.

So here are my friends, The Armstrongs. After reading this book I'm sure they'll become your friends too. Enjoy their amazing journey into the Heart of Rock and Roll.

John Dossett
Swamps of New Jersey, April, 2021

John Dossett is a Tony-nominated actor, for his role in Gypsy, *and a veteran of many Broadway and off-Broadway shows including* Pippin, Mamma Mia!, War Paint, *and of course* Newsies *as Joseph Pulitzer. His film and TV credits include* Man on a Ledge, Little Manhattan, Sex and the City *and HBO's* John Adams. *Furthermore, he is described by the authors of this book as perhaps the nicest guy on Earth.*

THE BAND TAKES THE STAGE

Introduction(s)

From the Daughter

During my freshman year in high school, the Rock and Roll Hall of Fame induction ceremony was held in Cleveland. With the city only a little over an hour from home in Warren, Ohio, my dad and I decided we weren't just going to go to the ceremony; we would also stake out the red carpet outside the VIP party at the museum a few nights beforehand.

As a long-suffering lover of bands that nobody else my age ever heard of, I was thrilled. (Classic rock may be cool now, but it was not when I was a ten-year-old whose favorite singer was Joan Jett.) I ended up bringing a few friends with me, huge fans of the band Green Day, which was being inducted that year. We borrowed my grandparents' van, drove up to the city, and settled in on the ground beside the stanchions.

While my friends and I waited, I overheard my dad's voice. He can make friends anywhere, so I wasn't surprised that he'd struck up a conversation with another man in line. The guy was a former teacher, just like my dad, and as I listened to snippets of their conversation, I realized he was also an avid concertgoer.

And then he said something that stuck with us ever since: "I've seen everyone from Aerosmith to ZZ Top."

At that point, we were pretty avid concertgoers ourselves. I grew up surrounded by music—one of my earliest memories is of drifting off to sleep in the car on a family vacation, the sounds of Frankie Valli and the Four Seasons echoing in my ears—and steeped in my parents' vastly different music tastes. Although my dad is only two years older than my mom, he's a hardcore classic rock buff while my mom loves '80s dance tunes; I'll never forget the look on his face when my mom associated the Clash with "Rock the Casbah" rather than "London Calling." But I picked up a mixture of their music and have loved everything, from the Doors to Donna Summer.

I attended my first concert when I was nine. It was Mannheim Steamroller who brought the Christmas album I loved to life before my eyes. I never looked back. I wanted to feel that kind of magic in the air over and over again.

And I did. From Yo Yo Ma when I was ten to Barry Manilow just a month before that day at the Rock Hall, my parents and I had seen almost a hundred concerts already. We were even tracking them—my mom scrapbooked, and I had a running Microsoft Word Document color-coded to show the inductees of various music halls of fame—but now we had the perfect descriptor: "Everyone from Aerosmith to ZZ Top." We adopted that line and used it every time we talked about concerts.

It's been almost five years since that day and now our concert total has passed the two hundred mark, not at all hindered by college or even my semester abroad. At the time, we weren't consciously trying to check off A through Z. We just saw our favorite bands, explored new venues, and traveled across many states in the process. There were constant surprises and unplanned special moments. The stories we collected turned into classics, recounted at dozens of dinners with friends and family.

We were inspired to actually write it all down thanks to *The Reading Promise* by Alice Ozma. My mom bought both of us copies for Father's Day one year, and we both read it in a single weekend. It reminded me of my childhood, too, with all the books that my parents read out loud to me, but then my dad suggested that we should do something similar with all of the concerts we attended. I was instantly on board.

The line we'd heard at the Rock Hall that day served as the perfect motif. As we drove to vacation spots (mostly for more concerts), we wrote down bullet-point lists of letters and memories in my iPhone notes app. We even developed a few ground rules: we had to have both seen the band, together, though of course we could include bands my dad saw without me before I was old enough to attend, provided he later saw them again with me. (But yes, I am still holding that one E Street Band concert over his head—I can't believe they played E Street Shuffle and I missed it.) Also, bands were categorized by the first letter of their title (for example, Cheap Trick is under C) and artists by their last names (for example, Neil Diamond is under D—though we do reserve the right to make exceptions for artists whose names are within the name of their band (for example, Huey Lewis & The News is under H).

We were excited to discover that without even trying, we'd knocked out most of the alphabet before the book was even conceived. The lone exceptions were Q, X, and I. Soon we had Billy Idol tickets for later that summer, had booked a trip to see Queen (while wondering aloud how we hadn't made it to one of their concerts before), and poked around on Google until we discovered the X Ambassadors playing the Cleveland House of Blues that upcoming November.

Eventually, we got to work on the book itself. It's been an incredible experience reliving these experiences with each chapter we write. It's been a great escape from whatever's going on in our lives, especially in the era of COVID-19 when we can't go to any concerts, as well as a refresher course on the bands we love. I can't tell you how many times I've started on a chapter just to exclaim, "Oh my god, I don't listen to this band enough."

I'm also reminded every day how much music can make a difference. It's brought me closer to my whole family, provided the soundtrack to the most important times in my life, and changed me for the better. As much as rock and roll is often dismissed or boiled down to its sex-and-drugs reputation, there's real power and meaning in this genre of music and kindness in its performers.

I hope it inspires you to seek out some musical memories of your own. It's not just concerts, either. The Rock and Roll Hall of Fame. Graceland. Even our car has provided the backdrop to some of my favorite moments. I'm also a huge fan of Broadway musicals and I have slowly convinced my dad to get on board, so this can extend to you even if your thing is more Annie than Aerosmith. The important thing is that you share your favorite music with the people you love. I guarantee it'll change your lives.

Now let's get this concert started!

—Moira

From the Dad

When I was a student at LaBrae High School, I met the love of my life. I always say that I was running a very important errand for a teacher when I ran into my sister in the hallway. She had a broken ankle at the time and was being escorted to her next class that day by her friend Kim. I knew then Kim was the one for me.

Kim would graduate in 1991, two years after me, and by 1997 we were married. Whenever we tell the story of how we met, Kim jokes I was probably skipping class. I maintain the important errand story.

As we set out building a life together, we were blessed to have a child. Our daughter Moira was born in April of 2000. Moira and Kim are the best things to have ever happened to me.

When Moira was born, I wanted to be an active part of her life. That aligned perfectly with another one of my dreams. I had wanted to become a social studies teacher ever since I was in middle school, and with Kim's encouragement and support, I left a job in the private sector to get that teaching degree. I would not only be able to pursue one of the best jobs in the world but also become a stay-at-home dad for nearly three years while I earned my degree and license to teach. This gave me the chance to spend much more time with Moira than I could have ever imagined.

We lived within walking distance of a park, and we took frequent trips there, often bringing along her cousins. We also frequently went to the local library where, just like Norm on Cheers, everybody knew her name. This time also gave me the opportunity to share my love of music with her.

I'd been a music fan for as long as I could remember. My mom, Debbie, was only fourteen when I was born, and while my biological father was not a part of my life, she met and married my adopted dad, Ken. He was the same age as my mom. I love both of them to this day, but with our age proximity, my relationship with my parents was more akin to that with an older brother and sister than traditional parents. A benefit of that was they listened to some awesome music. They loved what we now call classic rock and it was always alive and well in our house. Their turntable and eight-track player would deliver artists like Fleetwood Mac, Bruce

Springsteen, Eric Clapton, Meat Loaf, the Cars, Janis Joplin, and many more into my life, and I inherited their passion for the genre. While family finances never allowed for me to see live concerts as I was growing up, I will always remember my first concert thanks to a friend and his dad's generosity.

It was the mid-1980s and Kenny Loggins was all the rage. I was in middle school and my friend Frank had an extra ticket to see him live at Blossom Music Center. I was on top of the world thinking how lucky I was to get to go and see one of the hottest musicians around. Frank's seats turned out to be fourth-row center. Talk about a memorable first concert experience.

To this day, I always ask anyone I talk to about their first concert. That question always brings a smile to people's faces. Just like me, I think they love remembering who they saw, who brought them along, and the incredible memory of seeing the magic of a live performance for the very first time.

I wanted my time with Moira as she grew up to be meaningful to our family and to carry on from her childhood into her teenage years. Music was the perfect avenue. She has grown up listening to the same bands I did...with a few additions, of course. Kim's taste is more wide-ranging and includes '80s rock, dance music, and country.

The three of us have put many a mile on our Saturns, Ford Focus, and Lordstown-Ohio-built Chevy Cruze over the years, traveling to see concerts both near and far. Not only have we seen the legends of rock, but we've also gone to some of Kim's favorites. I still recall going to an Alabama concert with her. Moira and I felt so out-of-place as we were surrounded by a crowd of enthusiastic fans, including my wife, while we were completely lost. That situation repeated itself for me a few years later at a Cher concert...although Moira, who has adopted some of Kim's taste, was right there with the rest of the crowd on that one. Gypsies, Tramps, and Thieves... who knew?

Some people in our lives have scoffed at our choices to take Moira to rock and roll concerts, citing the grittier elements of the genre. In fact, when some find out that this is a love of ours, they're very surprised. But like any shared passion, the music has been a huge part of building a family bond that will last forever. Our love of classic rock goes hand in hand with the fun we have as a family. In the Jack Nicholson film *As Good As It Gets*, Nicholson tells Helen Hunt's character, "Some people have great stories, pretty stories that take place at lakes with boats and friends and noodle salad." Not sure why that stuck with us, as we are not lake or boat folk, but we took it as a way to sum up the good things in our lives. So despite the challenges life throws our way, we have tried to always be appreciative that we also had noodle salad.

As people told us would happen, Moira was through school and off to college before we knew it. However, we've continued our traditions: listening to music in the car, going to concerts, visiting the Rock Hall, and, now, writing this book. We've had an amazing time, although it was tough to choose just one band for each letter. I mean, come on—why do Jett (Joan), John (Elton), Joel (Billy), The J. Geils Band, and Journey all begin with the letter J? As a tribute and not to neglect the many bands we love, we've included an Outtakes section for each letter about some of the others we've been lucky enough to see over the years. We also have a section at the end, which we're calling our Encore, where we're listing some of the bands that remain on our dream concert list, which begs the questions: Will Cat Stevens ever return to the US? Will Billy Squier ever tour again?

We are excited to share our journey with you. Hope you enjoy our noodle salad memories with a soundtrack of rock and roll.

—Terry

Aerosmith TO ZZ TOP

A DAD & DAUGHTER'S ROCK & ROLL JOURNEY

AEROSMITH

August 7, 2015 at Tom Benson Hall of Fame Stadium in Canton, Ohio

Moira gets a picture of Steven Tyler of Aerosmith as we arrive at the Pro Football Hall of Fame

The year was 1997. It was the 7th Game of the World Series. Our local Cleveland Indians had the game won against the Florida Marlins—a triumph after the close loss in '95 to the Atlanta Braves. We hadn't had a championship since 1948, and as the victory came closer and closer, commentator Bob Costas started talking about the Indians I had watched growing up. I was so excited. I couldn't believe that after all this time, I was going to see my team win the World Series. The story goes that the trophy had already been taken to the Indians' locker room, banners were put up all around the

3

locker room in preparation for a huge celebration, and the MVP trophy already had Cleveland Indians pitcher Chad Ogea's name on it!

But then, the Marlins made a comeback. It was the most heart-breaking moment in a lifetime of watching Cleveland sports.

From that moment and many others (all of us Cleveland sports fans know Red Right 88, The Drive, The Fumble, and, for the Cavs, The Shot) to another World Series loss in 2016, Cleveland sports are not for the faint of heart. And although our family agrees on many things, my wife and daughter are not sports fans. I still recall coaching Moira in tee ball for a year. When the next season rolled around and I asked if she wanted to play again, she said in the nicest way possible, "No, thank you." She and Kim humor me as I watch my teams. They even take in an occasional game with me, but they prefer reading a good book to the goings-on at the Cleveland lakeshore or the corner of Carnegie and Ontario.

My friends always ask me, "Why would you even want to raise Moira as a Cleveland sports fan? I mean…they lose all the time." I always answer, "Being a Cleveland sports fan prepares you for disappointments in life." But being rooted in the Cleveland sports team tradition, I found it important to pass it on to Moira anyway. I thought the best chance I had with football was a historical connection: professional football originated in northeast Ohio, so we could tour the Pro Football Hall of Fame in nearby Canton. My friends and I had not only visited, but also attended the inductions and watched the annual parade a few times. But how would I convince Moira to go?

Little did I know our love of music would be just what would bring us to Canton together.

The weeklong induction festivities had always included many other fan-friendly events, and in 2015, they announced a new addition: a concert. When they announced that Aerosmith would be performing, I knew that this was my in.

Moira did want to go, and even agreed to head to Canton early so I could take her to the Hall of Fame itself. I couldn't wait to show her the eight championships won by the Cleveland Browns—eight that many non-Cleveland fans would point out occurred prior to the Super Bowl era, but I think they count just as much.

We parked the car and started heading towards the Football Hall of Fame, me telling a story about a previous visit as we walked.

"I was there with my friends for the inductions one year, walking around, and there he was: Jack Lambert, a Hall of Fame linebacker from our rival Pittsburgh Steelers. I was walking, he was walking, and we ran right into each other. But Jack Lambert didn't take me down."

Moira was smiling, humoring me as I told this story for the hundredth time, when suddenly she stopped in the middle of the sidewalk and exclaimed, "Is that Steven Tyler?"

I followed her gaze toward the road, and sure enough, there he was: the lead singer of Aerosmith, perched on the back of a golf cart! He looked pretty relaxed for a guy who was about to play a show for 23,000 people, just smiling and casually strumming a ukulele.

Moira's Memories

Yes, it's true. I'd heard it all before so I was more interested in looking around—and that's when I saw Steven Tyler!

Moira pulled out her cell phone, which she had gotten about a month earlier, and snapped a photo. It remains the first photo in her iPhone camera roll to this day. As we walked through the Hall of Fame, we both texted her amazing photo of rock royalty to everyone we knew.

The day had already far surpassed our expectations and we hadn't even gotten through the door of the venue yet. We were still buzzing with excitement as the ushers scanned our tickets. We picked up a concert t-shirt at the merch stand by the entrance, adding to our large collection, and then headed for our seats.

From the first notes of "Draw the Line," Aerosmith brought the house down. They sang all the hits with the same energy they did early in their careers. You never would have known that they were almost 70 years old!

As we watched, I thought back to high school. I had a friend named Mark who wore an Aerosmith t-shirt to school virtually every day. He was the biggest Aerosmith fan I had ever met, and now I understood exactly why he loved them so much.

They also paid tribute to some other Rock and Roll Hall of

Famers, covering the Beatles' "Come Together" and Fleetwood Mac's "Stop Messin' Around." Plus, we were reminded that they helped usher in the rap era with Run DMC as they teamed up with Living Colour, the opening act for the night, to play "Walk This Way."

At one point, during a bit of a lull in the action, we walked up to the concession stand for a bottle of water. It was situated on a hill behind the stage, and as we returned to our seats, we had an incredible view: we could see the crowd just like the band would be seeing them, a sea of people illuminated by the glow of stage lights.

The concert ended with a little surprise: Steven Tyler, known for his flamboyant stage wear, pulled off his jacket and tossed it into the crowd as the band finished up their encore, the iconic "Dream On"! We watched as a lucky fan caught it and laughed at the unexpected twist. Later, we found out that it was the last show of their 2015 North American tour—guess Steven didn't want to take that particular coat home.

While it was a last for Aerosmith, it was a first for us: Tom Benson Stadium was home to our first stadium show. And it was the first time Moira went *without complaint* to a sports landmark. It was a truly incredible day and a concert we still talk about every time "Sweet Emotion" comes on the radio.

—*Terry*

OUTTAKES

AC/DC
September 2016 at Nationwide Arena in Columbus, Ohio

AC/DC was on a list of bands that we had wanted to see for a long time. The tour did not feature lead singer Brian Johnson, which was disappointing, but Axl Rose of Guns N' Roses would be a great replacement. There was not much banter with the crowd, but the straight-on rock and roll did not disappoint. There were so many iconic songs that night, but the one that stands out in my mind is "Hells Bells," complete with a giant bell suspended over the stage with an echoing toll. We also thought it was hilarious that the one time Axl did interact with the audience was to tell us all how much he was enjoying Jeni's Ice Cream, which he apparently had a pint of backstage—it's a favorite of ours, too, just not what you expect to hear about mid-concert from such a hard rocker.

-Moira

Kim's Commentary

I remember our wedding reception and AC/DC blasting out at Roby Lees Banquet Hall much like at our high school dance days. Me and my friends danced the night away while Terry's crew chatted and played a little air guitar.

Bryan Adams
August 2019 at DTE Energy Center in Clarkston, Michigan

Kim and I saw Bryan Adams in Youngstown; his songbook, filled with classic ballads and energetic rock classics, spoke to both of us. He took us right back to the MTV years with Cuts Like a Knife and transported us to the movies with songs like "Everything I Do, I Do It For You." As '80s era high school sweethearts Bryan Adams is a romantic ballad legend. Unfortunately, Moira was not able to go, so when we heard that he was going to appear with Billy Idol in Michigan, we headed to the state up North for a double dose of '80s and '90s classics.

-Terry

Air Supply
October 2015 at Disney Epcot Eat to the Beat in Orlando, Florida

Every four years, my school's marching band takes a trip to Disney. This one was particularly memorable—there was a series of disasters, including a broken mirror that had to be duct-taped back to the bus and so many delays that we reached Orlando five hours later than originally planned—but we had a great time anyway. My dad chaperoned, and when we discovered that Air Supply was playing in Epcot's concert venue, we were immediately there! Our band also had a rule, established for safety purposes, that students had to be in groups of three at all times, so I ended up convincing two of my friends to go with me despite the fact that neither of them had ever heard of Air Supply. It was a short set, but it was filled with hits—"The One That I Love," "Even the Nights Are Better," and "I'm All Out of Love" among them. Just one more reason that Epcot is our favorite Disney park!   *-Moira*

Alabama
August 2013 at Playhouse Square in Cleveland, Ohio

We went to this concert for Mom, not knowing a single Alabama song. It was so different seeing a parking lot full of pickup trucks and a venue filled with cowboy hats and boots! But Mom loved it, so we did too—we were just taken aback when the crowd was yelling out "Sweet potato pie and shut my mouth."   *-Moira*

America
July 2014 at Ohio State Fairgrounds in Columbus, Ohio

America opened for the Beach Boys and played iconic songs such as "A Horse with No Name," "Sister Golden Hair," and "Ventura Highway." The perfect band to open for the Beach Boys. It always makes me think of Mr. Lendak, one of my incredible high school history teachers, who loved classic rock just as much as I did. As he passed back papers, he would make references to famous songs based on our names. He would call one of my classmates "Ventura Highway" since her last name was Ventura. Rock and roll lacks a "Moira"-oriented song or band so he honored me with the nickname "Joan Jett." Lendack was one of my favorite teachers ever and threw rock references in whenever he could.   *-Moira*

THE BEACH BOYS

September 2, 1984 at Canfield Fairgrounds in Canfield, Ohio

July 29, 2011 at DTE Energy Music Center in Clarkston, Michigan

July 29, 2014 at the Ohio State Fair in Columbus, Ohio

October 24, 2015 at Packard Music Hall in Warren, Ohio

In 1984, Kim and her family went to the Canfield Fair for that year's headline act: The Beach Boys. Their tickets were on the track, putting them right in front of the stage.

Unfortunately, that track soon turned into a sea of mud thanks to pouring rain.

That didn't deter them. Kim and her cousin Michele donned garbage bags and danced the night away to Mike Love singing the classic tracks. She remembers that they didn't sit down the entire night.

She had no idea at the time, but years later, she and our daughter would stand all night at another Beach Boys concert.

Our whole family are die-hard fans of the band. There's a Beach Boys song for every season, and you'll hear them echoing throughout our house or thumping through our car almost every day of the year. The iconic songs of summer, their Christmas tracks, and, of course, *Pet Sounds*, which we firmly believe is one of the greatest albums of all time.

In 2011, we took a family road trip up to Detroit to see one of their concerts at the DTE Energy Music Center. Moira was only eleven years old at the time and this was one of our first of many out-of-state trips to see bands who weren't soon coming to neighboring Cleveland, Pittsburgh, or Columbus.

Much like Blossom Music Center back home, this was an outdoor venue with a pavilion. And much like Blossom, a late July concert even at night was hot and humid.

Moira and her mom do not fare well in the heat. When Moira was little, we were playing in the town park as a family one day when she looked up at us and said, "I'm very humid." That sentiment was echoed years later, when she almost passed out at a marching band rehearsal and informed the director, "I don't do well in the heat. It's my Nordic blood!"

Despite the family joke that none of us enjoy temperatures above 70°, we overcame that for the Beach Boys! Kim and Moira danced all night to the classic Beach Boys tunes, not caring how hot and sweaty it was. And they sang so much they lost their voices the next morning!

Kim remembers that after the song "I Get Around," front man Mike Love joked, "If I said that to a girl now, she'd probably never have sex with me." Apparently, he'd said it the very first time she saw him in concert, too, and it must play well with audiences because he keeps telling it. The difference is that the band's age is now starting to show: Love now adds, "We are going to play you a few songs, take a nap, come back out for a few more, take another nap."

We traveled together to see the band again exactly three years later. Their new tour brought them to the Ohio State Fair in the state capital, a great venue for a concert. I found it particularly helpful when Moira was younger, as the Ohio State Highway Patrol provides security. They don't let anything out of the ordinary take place on their watch—a contrast for sure with the outdoor DTE Energy Center, where we frequently smelled marijuana throughout the concert. But that's never an issue at a venue patrolled by Ohio's finest. One less thing to worry about for Dad.

This trip took an unusual turn, though. I had gone down to an education conference the previous day, so Kim's parents drove Moira and Kim down to meet me at a rendezvous point: a Cracker Barrel north of Columbus, Ohio.

Over dinner at one of our favorite restaurants, I told them how odd I had been feeling lately. I had just felt tired the previous day and had brushed it off, but by that morning, it had turned into full-blown sickness. A pounding headache, complete exhaustion, and body aches all over, but especially my wrists and ankles. It was bizarre. But I decided I'd power through in pursuit of a great night at a rock concert.

Unfortunately, within a few hours, Kim and Moira came down with the same symptoms. We were supposed to see three nights of shows while in Columbus—the Beach Boys, Joan Jett with Heart, and Aretha Franklin—and couldn't imagine how we would do it. But that night, we dragged ourselves through a mile of the State Fair, past the smell of gyros, the sight of pig races, the line to see the cow made out of butter, and all the other joys of a State Fair midway.

When we arrived, we were very excited and surprised to see John Stamos join the band on guitar, vocals, and even drums during the night's concert. Apparently, he's a huge fan and sits in from time to time. And while we didn't have the energy for any dancing and singing along this time around, the rest of the crowd more than made up for it. They were full of energy, singing along at the top of their lungs, and even bouncing a few beach balls around.

As exhausted as we were, we did it again the next night, and the next, seeing both Joan Jett and Aretha. It was tough, but with the help of a few naps throughout the day, we didn't let the Columbus Crud keep us down.

Lastly, as fantastic as the two previous concerts were, there's nothing like a band you love coming to your hometown. The Beach Boys did just that in October of 2015 as they played the W. D. Packard Music Hall in Warren. Packard has had quite a resurgence as a local management company has taken it over with great success. The venue has been host to many dance recitals, high school grad-uations, and pro wrestling shows. This would be the beginning of a great tradition of rock bands playing Packard.

It also presented the opportunity to invite someone new along to join in our family concert adventures. Just like my friend Frank took me to my first concert, Moira was able to take her friend Adam to his very first. It became only the first of many times she was able to introduce someone to this part of her world.

I forget sometimes how unique it is that Moira loves classic rock and has seen so many concerts and live bands. Many kids her age don't appreciate the classic rock genre...or think they don't like it because they haven't seen a live band to understand how great it is. But Adam enjoyed the iconic band serenading our hometown just as much as we did, and we were glad to have him with us at what became our favorite Beach Boys concert yet. Though October in Northeast Ohio is more known for leaf peeping and a first sign of snow, the Beach Boys gave us all a dose of Surfin' USA that night.

—Terry

OUTTAKES

The Baseball Project
July 2019 at the Rock and Roll Hall of Fame in Cleveland, Ohio

In 2019, one of my dad's dreams came true: the Major League Baseball All Star Game returned to Cleveland and we got to go. Dad is a huge baseball fan and loves the Cleveland Indians in particular. We attended tons of the tie-in events throughout the city, including this concert, which starred Scott McCaughey and Steve Wynn of R.E.M. and featured songs about baseball that my dad loved! The song "The Straw that Stirs the Drink" is still in his head, bringing back memories for him of Reggie Jackson. *-Moira*

Pat Benatar
June 2016 at Heinz Hall in Pittsburgh, Pennsylvania

Pat Benatar was part of the dream triple bill that Moira and I constantly dream about but has not happened yet: Joan Jett, Cyndi Lauper, and Pat Benatar. Pat has so many iconic songs and this night we would not only get to see her perform them with her husband (and Cleveland-born) Neil Giraldo but also, incredibly, backed by the Pittsburgh Symphony Orchestra. We still look forward to the dream triple bill but on that night, Pat, Neil, and the orchestra were all fired up! *-Terry*

Tony Bennett
October 2011 at Playhouse Square in Cleveland, Ohio

This is one I still can't believe we got to see, especially as we have lost many of the major names from this era. We actually got to see one of the major classic crooners live in one of our favorite theaters. Classics like "I Left my Heart in San Francisco," "Fly Me to the Moon," and "Rags to Riches" filled the night with music from days gone by and left us still talking about it weeks, months, and even years later. We also got to see Mr. Bennett's daughter Antonia, both as a solo performer and doing a great duet with her dad.

I remember that when we were on our way into the theatre, one of the Playhouse Square ushers tried to make a joke. We call the ushers the "Red Coats" as they wear bright red blazers. They have been the subjects of many Revolutionary War jokes from my dad and I. The Red Coat who scanned our tickets at the door joked about how young I was, though she didn't quite hit the mark when she asked me if I was there to see Bon Jovi or Def Leppard! Not exactly my demographic as a middle schooler in 2011 but you gotta love those Red Coats! *-Moira*

Blondie
June 2015 at Packard Music Hall in Warren, Ohio

Blondie kicked off this tour at Madison Square Garden...and then came straight to Warren, Ohio for the second stop on the tour! It was so cool picking up a t-shirt where New York City was followed directly by Warren. Walking into a venue we know very well, the Packard Music Hall, we saw many out of state license plates; many fans were following the band on the road as they do not tour often. We were lucky to be hosting Blondie in our own hometown and they put on a great show to a sold-out crowd. And every time I was on that stage afterwards, from dance recitals to high school graduation, I thought about how I was standing in the very place that Blondie had been. *-Moira*

Blue Oyster Cult and Bachman Turner Overdrive (with Foghat)
July 2014 at the Ohio State Fairgrounds in Columbus, Ohio

Not only a great triple bill but two of them begin with "B"! Blue Oyster Cult proved to be much more than just "more cowbell." "Don't Fear the Reaper," "Burning for You," and "Godzilla" brought everyone to their feet, singing along to those classic lyrics—but also enjoying the cowbell interlude, of course!

Bachman Turner Overdrive gives us great memories as a family. "Takin' Care of Business" was the mantra of the person to first connect Moira to rock and roll (outside of her parents): Elvis Presley. Kim often reminds me how often I would play BTO when I had my first apartment (classic one bedroom above a garage). As often happened when I would introduce her to music that was new to her, she enjoyed it. Great concert and those standing up during Blue Oyster Cult decided to just continue standing the entire night for classic rock and roll.

-Terry

Jason Bonham/Led Zeppelin Experience (with Foreigner and Cheap Trick)
July 2017 Giant Center in Hershey, Pennsylvania

Although we missed out on seeing the original Led Zeppelin, we were excited when John Bonham's son, Jason Bonham, was bringing the Led Zeppelin Experience to Hershey, Pennsylvania as the opening act for Foreigner and Cheap Trick. We were in eastern Pennsylvania for a college visit to Swarthmore near Philadelphia. Stopping and seeing two bands we love and a chance to see the closest thing to Led Zeppelin out there was a no-brainer. We were just a little surprised when the lead singer broke out some Art of War Tai Chi style dancing during the night but Bonham on the drums rocked the night away. What a tribute to a legendary rock band.

-Terry

Boston
August 2012 at the Ohio State Fairgrounds in Columbus, Ohio

Boston proved they are not just another band out of Boston. I love the song "More than a Feeling" and could not wait to hear them play it as well as their other hits. I have so many memories of driving around with Boston playing—first on the radio, then cassette tapes, then CDs! In Northeast Ohio, we still have a rather robust classic rock radio presence. Legendary stations like WMMS out of Cleveland, long-standing juggernaut Y103 out of Youngstown, CD 93.3 (formerly CD106) out of Youngstown, relative newcomer Z104 out of Youngstown, Pittsburgh's WDVE 102.5, Cleveland's 106.5 (they play a lot of classic rock with the addition of their tagline "We play anything"), 98.5 WNCX out of Cleveland, and 97.5 WONE also out of Cleveland are just some examples of a lasting rock and roll music scene coming from terrestrial radio.

I remember one time working the last day at a job I knew I would miss and putting on Y103 on as I left and Boston's "Don't Look Back" came on. It is true you can mark times in your life with music. They did not disappoint when we saw them and I can't wait to see them again and get lost in every familiar song.   *-Terry*

Jim Brickman (with Tracy Silverman)
November 2010 at KSU Tuscarawas Art Center in New Philadelphia, Ohio

My dad was so excited to take my mom and I to see the world-renowned pianist Jim Brickman. While he was great, we were enamored with the hilarious and talented electric violin player, Tracy Silverman, and went home with his CDs and plans to see him perform again! Jim Brickman, a native Clevelander, is a wonderful talent as well but Dad is still not over the fact that we latched onto the violinist.   *-Moira*

Garth Brooks
October 2015 at Quicken Loans Arena in Cleveland, Ohio

Instead of going to homecoming sophomore year, I spent the day in Cleveland with my family: we went to the Rock Hall, took in an early evening performance of Potted Potter (a Harry Potter parody show), and then saw Garth Brooks' late night show (he did two in one night) at Quicken Loans Arena, or the Q. It was a great day in one of our favorite cities! We always say Cleveland is to New York as Columbus is to Washington, DC. Garth Brooks capped things off with a great show. We have the CD collection that features his covers of classic rock songs... if you have not listened to it you must check it out! A few years later in college, I recounted this story to some new friends who hadn't known me back then, and while they weren't surprised that I passed on a dance for a day in Cleveland, they were completely shocked when I told them who it was. One even joked, "did you wear your cowboy boots?" only for me to respond honestly, "Yes."   *-Moira*

Jackson Browne
June 2016 at the Akron Civic Theater in Akron, Ohio

Jackson Browne proved to be the singer/song-writer folk-singing legend we thought he would be. I have always been a fan of "Running on Empty" and "Lawyers in Love" as well as a song I knew Moira would enjoy, partly because it is a good up-beat song but it also is a duet Browne did with the E Street Band's Clarence Clemmons, "You're a Friend of Mine." We were also excited to see, when we became involved with the TeachRock initiative, that he's a huge advocate for the arts in schools.   *-Terry*

CHEAP TRICK

**August 8, 2015 at the Ohio State Fair in Columbus, Ohio
(with Peter Frampton)**

**July 22, 2016 at the Riverbend Music Center in Cincinnati, Ohio
(with Joan Jett and Heart)**

**July 15, 2017 at the Giant Center in Hershey, Pennsylvania
(with Foreigner and Jason Bonham)**

Moira and Terry backstage with Cheap Trick

When I was ten years old, my Uncle Ted, a huge music fan just like me, said to me, "I want to buy everyone an album for Christmas this year." I was so excited—I scoured the shelves of records at Hills Department store, trying to decide what album I would ask for. Finally, I decided on *The Rock Album* by K-Tel. K-Tel released compilation albums that I saw advertised on TV all the time and I thought getting one would be the best. It had all the hits—"Two Tickets to Paradise," "Renegade," "Carry On Wayward Son"—I couldn't wait to listen to them all.

Ripping the wrapping paper off that album on Christmas morning felt like I was winning the lottery. I immediately took it up to my room when I got home, where I had my own turntable, and listened to the album all the way through. I loved every song on it, but there was one I kept returning to "Dream Police" by Cheap Trick.

It wasn't easy to find a specific song on an album like it is on Spotify or a CD. You had to pick up the needle and set it down carefully on the ridges, looking for the exact spot where the song started. My fellow Gen X'ers, and boomers before us, will back me up that sometimes you would have a skip to deal with too. The only appropriate antidote was balancing a dime on the needle. I did it over and over. "Dream Police" and much of *The Rock Album* had burrowed into my brain.

I still have this album in my collection, and it brings back many memories of being alone in my room, spinning vinyl for escape and enjoyment. Cheap Trick remained a part of my life as they made it big on MTV in the 1980s. My friends and I, living in the city of Warren, were able to keep up with their music and videos now in our living rooms.

Kim, on the other hand, often reminds us that where she grew up in the country they had no cable and thus no MTV. When I mention certain videos from my childhood and she has no clue what I'm talking about, she defends this by pointing out that they had Friday night videos...which is a far cry from the continuous loop of music that MTV brought me.

I remember as MTV started to transition to more programming beyond music videos, they had a game show called *Remote Control*. One of the contests was called "Sing Along with Colin." Every time I remember this I recall my now brother-in-law Travis, who was dating my sister, had a propensity to sing the classic rock tunes out loud. This resulted in my dad calling the game "Sing Along with Trav."

Back in 2015, Moira and I traveled to the Ohio State Fair to see a double bill of Cheap Trick and Peter Frampton. Frampton was the headliner and quite frankly I was equally excited to see both of them. In the car on the way to Columbus, Moira pointed out how often I mentioned the album *Frampton Comes Alive*. I told her stories about how big Frampton's hits were in my house growing up. "I can't wait to see him sing and play the guitar like, well, like only he does."

What neither of us were prepared for was Cheap Trick.

We walked in, found our seats, and took a quick selfie with the stage in the background. It was a special occasion—Moira's 100th concert—so we celebrated with front-row seats.

Before the show began, a voiceover announced, "Ladies and gentlemen. Please welcome to the stage...the best effing band you'll ever see live...Cheap Trick."

I hate to say that we were skeptical, but we were. I loved listening to them, but how on earth were they going to cash that check?

Well, they did that and more. They rocked the whole building with "Surrender," "I Want You to Want Me," "The Flame," and of course, my old K-Tel favorite "Dream Police." The eye contact and attentiveness to the crowd was outstanding. We completely understood the many loyal fans we saw, dressed up in police outfits and who had spent their summers following the band as they toured the country. It was an electric crowd and we were thrilled to be there. We were even more thrilled that we walked away with about half a dozen guitar picks from Rick Nielsen, who flicked them into the crowd at a furious pace.

Although we always try to add new bands to our concert schedule, there are some favorites that we can't stay away from. Cheap Trick quickly became one of those bands that we would see over and over because we loved seeing them live so much. A year later, we traveled to the Riverbend Center in Cincinnati for an incredible triple bill. Cheap Trick, Joan Jett and the Blackhearts, and Heart.

It was a long trip. Cincinnati and Warren may be in the same state, but we're in Northeast Ohio about fifteen minutes away from the PA border and Cincinnati is over four hours away, sharing a border (and many residents) with Kentucky. But nothing could stop us from a trio of Rock Hall inductees.

After this show, we bought the Meet and Greet package. We had never done this before for any artist and they did not disappoint. As soon as we stepped under the white tent, guitarist Rick Nielsen was standing ready to greet us. He called out, "Look, guys, its Joan Jett!" pointing out Moira's t-shirt.

We joined the rest of the band on a couch, where we snapped a few pictures and chatted. We talked about music and Moira mentioned her school band. Robin Zander asked her what instrument she played. When she responded, "Alto saxophone," he said, "Well, we'll keep you in mind if we ever need to hire someone on sax."

The Meet and Greet came along with fantastic seats as well and Cheap Trick again did not disappoint.

In July 2017, their bassist Tom Peterson took things to an entirely new level. By then, it was time to take Moira on college campus visits. She would eventually seriously consider sixteen colleges on her quest for the right one. I thought this was perfect, as for her graduation party I was able to take all sixteen in consideration and make a bracket tournament showing the progression of her choice. This would be one of my contributions for her graduation party... an addition my friends loved by the way. And of course we had one of our favorite local bands play as well: Black Wolf and the Thief.

One of the colleges she was considering was Swarthmore near Philadelphia, Pennsylvania. Swarthmore did not end up being the right place for Moira. The tour guide opened the session by saying, "If at any point during this presentation you decide Swarthmore isn't for you, you can leave." She then informed us that students aren't allowed to declare a major right away, and told us what was supposed to be a funny anecdote about how one student declared a math major so he could take more English classes due to their academic structure. Moira was so disturbed

The next thing I knew she stood up and left the room. I just wish she'd had let me know, as I was still sitting there with all the other parents and prospective students. I did then check in with her via text and found out she was taking the guide up on the earlier offer to leave as soon as she realized this was not for her.

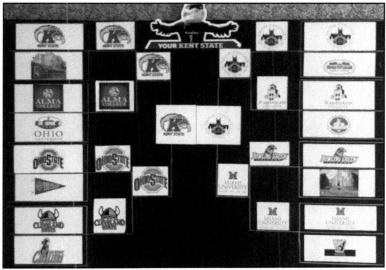

College Visit Bracketology - Moira's path to Kent State
(Left side: Kent State University, Case Western Reserve University, Alma College,
Ohio University, Ohio State University, Oberlin College, Cleveland State University,
Walsh University. Right side: Smith College, Swarthmore College, Randolph College,
Malone University, Bowling Green State University,
University of Pittsburgh, Miami of Ohio. and College of Wooster.)

Though a nice campus and I'm sure great for some, it did not make it out of the first round of the Moira College Choice Bracket Tournament.

Luckily, the trip wasn't all bad. As luck would have it, on our way back home, Cheap Trick was playing with Foreigner at the Giant Center in Hershey. So of course, we went.

We purchased tickets for the front row. They were significantly cheaper than the other tickets in the front with the warning of an obstructed view. But we thought, "How bad can it be? It's the front row!"

Well, when we arrived, there was our answer. In front of our seats were seven-foot speakers. If we turned a bit to the right, we could see the stage perfectly, but we were a little worried about just how loud this concert was going to be from these seats.

Kim is a speech pathologist and she always encourages us to wear earplugs. Of course we never listen and choose to instead just deal with the threshold shift, which affects me for days though Moira's young ears bounce back quicker. But tonight, we were a little worried.

Luckily, the most unexpected person came to our rescue: Cheap Trick bassist Tom Peterson.

In addition to the speakers, the sound control board was just to our left, and behind that, a path led to backstage. While we were in our seats, waiting for the concert to begin, Tom Peterson walked out to take a look around. He started chatting with us and pointed out that we were sitting right in front of the massive speakers.

"I hope you brought earplugs." he laughed. "I think you're going to need them."

I shook my head. "No, we didn't bring any."

"Well, if I get you some, will you wear them?"

We of course said yes, and he disappeared for a while. We had a snack, looked around, and talked about what songs we hoped the band would play. Just before they took the stage, Mr. Peterson returned.

"You thought I forgot about you." he said, holding out two sets of earplugs and a few guitar picks. "Enjoy the show."

We thanked him profusely and settled down to enjoy the concert. Our luck continued; the two seats next to us remained empty throughout the night and we eventually moved out from behind the speakers entirely!

Mr. Peterson continued to prove that he hadn't forgotten about us. In the middle of one of the numbers, he walked over to us, pointed, and mouthed, "Are they working?" We cheered in response. By the end of the night, we had even more guitar picks and even Foreigner's setlist, handed to Moira by a roadie.

We're always astonished by Robin Zander, who manages to make eye contact with everyone in the audience no matter where they sit, really driving home the feeling that they are playing just for you. We love Rick Nielsen's little gestures, flicking his guitar picks and tossing a record during Surrender, and pointing sideways to his bandmates. And of course, Tom Peterson has a special place in our hearts. No matter what, we will always believe that Cheap Trick really is the best effing band you will ever see live.

—Terry

OUTTAKES

Cher (with Cyndi Lauper)
May 2014 at Quicken Loans Arena in Cleveland, Ohio

Cher has been on Kim and Moira's bucket list from the beginning. While I know her earlier stuff such as "Gypsies, Tramps and Thieves," Kim and Moira like her more modern pop and dance music. What a night. She changed outfits constantly and even was transported throughout the arena by air. She put on a wonderful show and sang all of her hits. I could see that night why she had such a following and loved seeing Kim and Moira having such a great time. Cyndi Lauper was a great opening act and Moira will share some other highlights of the night when she talks about Cyndi later in the book.   -*Terry*

Kim's Commentary

Cher had the crowd going from the start but no more than the clapping of the hands during Dark Lady. The song is perfect for that kind of crowd participation...we even got Terry to join in!

Chicago
February 2016 at Packard Music Hall in Warren, Ohio

Chicago is the horn-driven rock band that we had hoped. Seeing them in Warren was perfect as Moira, Kim, and I sang along to so many classic songs that night, joined by many we knew in the crowd. Hits like "Saturday in the Park," 25 or 6 to 4," and "Feeling Stronger Every Day." Crowd response was great as this band sounded just as we have heard them on the radio, vinyl, CD, and streaming. -*Terry*

Alice Cooper
May 2016 at Packard Music Hall in Warren, Ohio

Alice Cooper also would come to our hometown of Warren, Ohio. I always enjoyed his more popular songs—"Schools Out," "No More Mr. Nice Guy," and "I'm Eighteen"—but my experience of his music is rather limited and clearly more limited than those that joined us in the audience. I did enjoy him taking his turn at acting in *Wayne's World*—"We're not worthy!" His stage shows are legendary, and this was on display right there at Packard Music Hall. -*Terry*

Elvis Costello
July 2015 at Blossom Music Center in Cuyahoga Falls, Ohio

Elvis Costello was opening for Steely Dan at the outdoor concert venue in the Cleveland area. We had certainly heard of Elvis Costello but were not too familiar with his music. He had great stage presence and you could see and hear why he had such a following. We had an odd connection to him as our whole family are fans of the show *Frasier*. One episode features Elvis Costello as a house musician at their coffee house hangout Café Nervosa. Frasier decides to boycott because he finds the music annoying, but his brother Niles can't stand any of the new shops they try, so he sneaks back in—only to have Elvis Costello bring him into the act shaking a maraca. Of course, he's dancing around with it when Frasier walks in and catches him! He was as hilarious as he was entertaining that night at the Blossom Music Center. -*Terry*

CCR/Creedence Clearwater Revisited
April 2012 at Quicken Loans Arena in Cleveland, Ohio
November 2013 at Quicken Loans Arena in Cleveland, Ohio

We saw CCR (Credence Clearwater Revisited) for the first time at the Moondog Coronation Ball in Cleveland. This version of CCR was minus John Fogerty but maintained their quality and presence with original members Stu Cook and Doug "Cosmo" Clifford. The crowd, who had been fairly subdued for the first few acts, absolutely exploded when they took the stage! Their portion of the show was electric and filled with our favorite songs. We later would see John Fogerty live as a solo act but lead singer Bulldog held his own connecting with the crowd at the Q.

We have listened to their songs over and over again and to see it live and with a high energy crowd made this night very special. CCR has always been a favorite of mine because they defy categorization, with music that combines blues and swamp rock and almost-country with the hard rock we like so much. But despite their country roots and imagery, they're antiwar and anti-establishment, and performed at Woodstock—very unlike other country or country-influenced groups at the time.

They were part of my inspiration for an assignment I would assign in my government class called "Democracy Rocks." Students would be assigned to select a song that had a social commentary, write an analysis of the song, and create an original album cover (after explaining to some what an album is). I would often use CCR's "Fortunate Son" as an example to share with the class as we would dissect the song in class. This was one of my favorite assignments to work with students and CCR was the perfect lead-in...as was their rendition of "Have You Ever Seen the Rain" that night at Quicken Loans Arena.   -*Terry*

NEIL DIAMOND

July 1, 2012 at Quicken Loans Arena in Cleveland, Ohio

March 18, 2015 at the Schottenstein Center in Columbus, Ohio

May 30, 2017 at Quicken Loans Arena in Cleveland, Ohio

Kim and Moira at Neil Diamond concert in Cleveland

No experience is more universal than Neil Diamond.

When I was in high school, I played alto saxophone in the marching band. Freshman year, our show (themed Viva Las Vegas) concluded with "Sweet Caroline"—we created four giant circles on the field, which expanded and contracted, and then formed a giant kick line from end zone to end zone. The community calls it "150 yards of marching Tigers" and remained one of my favorite drills until I graduated.

We kept the song around as a stand tune. We often broke it out at breaks between quarters when we had a little longer to play a song; we also had a teacher, Mr. O'Neil, who requested it at every single pep rally. As I stood in formation, I would always see him tapping his foot and singing along up in the stands. And he wasn't the only one.

Moira's high school band

From Boston Red Sox fans to die-hard music lovers, everyone knows the words to "Sweet Caroline." Though nobody had heard of most of the bands whose concert t-shirts I wore to school, all I had to do was mention that song and instantly, Neil Diamond was recognized.

He was a household favorite, too. My mom owned the CD of *Hot August Night*, a live concert album, and we listened to it on so many real-life hot August nights that I learned to recognize the songs by just the cheers at the beginning. By the time I was ten I knew every one of the classics by heart: "Forever in Blue Jeans." "Cracklin' Rosie." "Cherry Cherry." "You Don't Bring Me Flowers." And when I finally got an iPod, the first album I bought was the brand-new *Melody Road*.

When we bought tickets to see him for the first time, we were all so excited. But unfortunately health was not on my mom's side. She was sick and couldn't come with us.

The show was taking place at Cleveland's Quicken Loans Arena, or the Q. My parents not only brought me there frequently, but also saw many events there before I was born—though often in a previous incarnation. Prior to becoming the Q, it opened as Gund Arena in 1994 as part of a renaissance taking place in Cleveland's downtown. Prior to opening, the Richfield Coliseum was Northeast Ohio's major arena for concerts and sporting events. But the Coliseum was well outside the city, sitting by itself at a random exit 30 minutes away. Opening an arena downtown was part of Cleveland's plans to revitalize the city, a successful transformation that continues to draw us to Cleveland to this day.

Though I have heard my parents and their friends often talk about missing the old Richfield Coliseum, our family quickly fell in love with what would eventually become Quicken Loans Arena. Before I was born, my mom and dad saw everything there, from Scott Hamilton doing a backflip on ice to Bret Hart taking on Jerry "The King" Lawler in a rasslin ring! It is a tradition in the Midwest for high schoolers attending prom to go on an adventure of sorts the day after. Some head to amusement parks like Cedar Point, some to a campsite; my mom and dad spent the day at the zoo and headed that evening to the World Wrestling Federation show at the Richfield Coliseum.

Once I was around they took me to *Nemo on Ice* along with my older cousin Destiny. We still laugh as apparently I was so scared of the huge fish on ice while Destiny could not get enough. That was not the norm for me as Mom and Dad always said I did well with Santa, Easter Bunny, and also Scrappy, the mascot for our local minor league team, the Mahoning Valley Scrappers. But apparently over-sized sea life was a step too far.

Despite my mom not being able to attend this time to see Neil Diamond, it still proved an incredible night. Tears pricked in my eyes as he opened with "Coming to America," accompanied by images from Ellis Island. I love the story of his grandmother coming to the United States as a young girl, inspired by the American

Dream. He had great energy as he performed all the hits; plus, I was surprised to learn that he'd written the Monkees classic "I'm A Believer" and intended it as a ballad. As he strummed his guitar and quietly sang the familiar lyrics, our side of the arena burst into cheers. He grinned up at us.

"This side seems to like it very much," he remarked, walking our way as he moved into the next verse.

And of course, I'll never forget the first time I heard the iconic "Sweet Caroline" live. An entire arena singing along. Fists pumping in the air in sync to "So good! So good! So good!" It was one of the most magical music moments of my life.

But the great memories of that night only made us more determined to bring my mom. We were thwarted again in 2015 when we tried to go to a concert together again, this time in Columbus. But finally, in 2017, all three of us finally ended up chanting "So good!" together in the stands back at the Q. My mom, who had first introduced me to Neil, finally got to see him live.

I was heartbroken to hear the news that he was diagnosed with Parkinson's and would be retiring. I remember telling a friend about the many times we'd gone to his concerts and again I found that Neil was universal; she instantly knew who he was when I mentioned

It may not be at Quicken Loans Arena,
but Terry and Moira try their hands in the wrestling ring

"Sweet Caroline." He has been bringing people together for as long as he's been in the music business, and I'm so glad that even though he can't perform, his songs will always be immortalized—whether through the sound system at Fenway Park or the Howland marching band.

—*Moira*

OUTTAKES

The Diamonds
September 2011 at Packard Music Hall in Warren, Ohio

The Diamonds performed as a part of the Warren Civic Music Association's concert series in our hometown. My grandparents joined my mom and I. This was one my dad could not make. We really enjoyed the night with hits like "Little Darlin" and "The Stroll." Their CD became a staple of my playlist for a long time. *-Moira*

The Doobie Brothers
June 2016 at Blossom Music Center in Cuyahoga Falls, Ohio

The Doobie Brothers were the opening act for Journey this night in the outdoor concert venue for those in the Cleveland area. "Black Water," "Takin it to the Streets," "China Grove," and their finale "Listen to the Music" all rocked the crowd. It seemed the entire crowd was singing along to each and every song. One day we were visiting the Rock Hall and saw members of the Doobie Brothers walking around. Typically, Moira would have gone up to them, but Mom talked some sense into us, saying to leave them be and respect their privacy. While we complied, we both admit had Kim not been there Moira would have gone right up to them. And if past classic rocker responses are any indication, they would have been enamored with the fact that someone so young knew them and their music. *-Terry*

BRUCE SPRINGSTEEN &
THE E STREET BAND

**April 17, 2012 at Quicken Loans Arena in Cleveland, Ohio
(Terry only…sorry Moira)**

November 1, 2012 at Bryce Jordan Center in State College, Pennsylvania

February 23, 2016 at Quicken Loans Arena in Cleveland, Ohio

September 11, 2016 Consol Energy Center in Pittsburgh, Pennsylvania

Moira gets a sign ready for Bruce and the E Street Band concert

If you've ever been to a Bruce Springsteen concert, you know that you are in for more of an experience than a show or concert. They never, ever disappoint. You also know you're in for 3-plus hours of the "Heart-stopping, pants-dropping, house-rocking, earth-quaking, booty-shaking, Viagra-taking, love-making, legendary E Street Band!" every night they take the stage.

31

In that spirit, this may be the longest chapter of our A-Z journey through rock. Moira may rival me when she gets going about Elvis or Joan Jett, but Bruce and the band stop for no one!

Bruce and the band's songs resonated with me at every turn in my life, but it took me forty-one years to see them live. I inherited my passion for all things E Street from my dad, who loved their music because they sang the struggles of his generation and the working-class community we had in the Mahoning Valley.

We lost my dad to cancer in January of 2012 at fifty-six years young. This wasn't long after the E Street Band lost the Big Man, saxophonist Clarence Clemons. When the next tour came through Cleveland in April, Kim told me, "you have to go."

At this point, I have to apologize to Moira. She's a third-generation fan and wanted to go but she was only twelve years old and I was a little worried about taking her with me. I thought she might be too young to be among the huge, passionate crowd in the pit. I was wrong—not about the crowd being huge and passionate, but to doubt that she belonged among them. It will forever haunt me. Mostly because she won't let me forget it.

Instead, I took a friend of mine that I graduated from high school with, worked with, and still hang out with to this day. Rob was the perfect concert buddy: he was just as excited as I was as we headed to downtown Cleveland, and he was notoriously cheap. He would hang out in the pit with me the entire night so we wouldn't lose our spot on the crowded Quicken Loans Arena Floor, not just because of a passion for Bruce, but also because of his refusal to buy overpriced beer and snacks. (I knew this from experience: he proved his mettle in forever frugality at a Football Hall of Fame Ceremony, when, despite the 100-degree heat, he hunted for a water fountain rather than pay for a bottle of water. We tease him relentlessly for it sometimes, but you must admire his convictions.)

We had a fantastic time that night. I was jumping up and down with a fist in the air when he opened with "Badlands"—that is my MO (modus operandi) when that song is played live, Moira tells me. He then powered through several songs from the *Wrecking Ball* album, which was new at the time and the namesake for this particular tour; it was full of working-class anthems.

He also played "E Street Shuffle," a rarity at live concerts. I was thrilled, and the whole crowd clearly agreed as they created a conga line through the pit.

And of course, anyone who saw Bruce and the band in the years after the passing of Clarence Clemons are lying to you if they say they didn't shed a tear during "Tenth Avenue Freeze Out." I know I did. Clarence was Moira's favorite member of the band and the reason she chose to play alto saxophone when it came time to sign up for band. When we introduced her to the band with their version of "Santa Claus is Coming to Town," I also showed her the albums my dad had given me, and she loved the iconic *Born to Run* with Clarence and Bruce on the cover.

Moira's Memories

Let the record show that I did not attend this concert and still have not seen him play the E Street Shuffle! A bit of a sore subject with me other than my dad has to keep taking me to see Bruce until I see him and the band play it.

I recounted the concert with Moira the next day and saw the look on her face when I told her that they'd played her favorites, like "E Street Shuffle," that weren't exactly concert staples. I realized that I needed to take her next time the tour came nearby.

That November was our chance. We were so excited and spent weeks in advance doing recon—short for reconnaissance—which became the norm for our rock concerts and trips. It just means researching travel and concert logistics to find out everything that's going on, so we don't miss out. For this, it meant discovering that since we had pit tickets, we needed to show up very early, get a numbered wristband, and wait to hear a number from the event staff. The person with that numbered wristband would go into the arena first.

We headed for Penn State University's campus well in advance. It's quite a process, and as it all unfolded, we realized that most of the people around us were experienced concertgoers. Despite the fact that we were all technically competing for the best spaces in the pit, they were all very nice—helping explain the process to us, wishing us luck, and marveling that my twelve-year-old daughter was a fan of Bruce and the band. We met people who had been to a handful of concerts and people who had seen him dozens of times.

Some came from across the country, some from across campus. One group of guys had been following the band from town to town. Their t-shirts had a list of their stops, written in Sharpie, and they were checking off each one as their trip progressed. Each person was nicer than the last. Even the staff was great—our favorite was the guy running the wristband distribution and selection, who we nicknamed "Elvis Costello Guy" because of his striking resemblance to the iconic rocker.

When the time came for the drawing, we were so lucky: we would be two of the first ten people on the concert floor, setting off a chain celebration throughout our segment of the line. We were cheering and hugging total strangers as the staff ushered us into the arena corridors. As we waited with our Bruce and the E Street Band brethren, they shared their concert stories and experience with us, giving us tips on what to do when we were allowed in.

"Run like hell," one guy advised us.

"Find a spot you like, because you'll be there for the next five hours," another said.

"If you want to see Stevie and Garry, you want the right side. On the left, you'll have Jake and Nils," a third advised.

Moira and I, despite the fact that we're more mathletes than athletes, were more than ready for the challenge. The soundcheck echoed through the hallways, pumping us up. I still think about how I felt at that moment, bringing my daughter and knowing that we would be so close to the band.

Soon, the doors opened, inviting us onto the arena floor. And we took the advice of the guy in line: we ran like hell! We positioned ourselves in the very front, pressed against the right side of the stage. Soon, the space around us filled. There were so many people with Jersey accents that you would have thought we were in the Meadowlands, not State College, PA.

Moira sat on the floor and chatted with the friendly crowd around us while we waited for the action to start. I talked to the people around me as well and really hit it off with the security guard stationed nearby.

A few hours later, the lights dimmed. Moira leapt up from her place on the floor. We were on the edge of our seats, metaphorically of course, as the band exploded onto the stage. The opening number? "Lion's Den," in honor of the Penn State Nittany Lions. They don't miss anything.

They were still on their *Wrecking Ball* tour and continued heavily featuring songs from the album. I still remember the roadies dragging out a huge gong for "American Land" and Moira next to me cheering as they started the concert.

Our spot proved perfect over and over. We were perched directly in front of a platform that jutted out from the stage and Bruce walked out there many times throughout the show. One of the highlights was during "Spirit in the Night," when he not only shook our hands, but laid down right next to us to sing to a woman who was celebrating her 60th birthday. Soon, Jake Clemons joined him, and quickly proved that he had his uncle's talent. He clearly meshed perfectly with the rest of the band—Bruce had even nicknamed him "Jakie," kind of ironic because the saxophonist towered over the lead singer.

We had a perfect view for our favorite songs—"Backstreets," "Badlands," "Because the Night," "Born to Run," and "Rosalita." Moira and I still talk about how Stevie Van Zandt and Bruce played off each other throughout the song, with Stevie acting out many of the lines and downright cackling into the mic on the line, "Someday we'll look back on this and it will all seem funny."

The night was already exciting and special. But it was about to get even better. The band began "Dancing in the Dark," which has become iconic ever since the 1984 video with Courtney Cox dancing onstage with the Boss. This happens night after night as the band tours, a girl or two getting the opportunity to hop onstage and dance with Bruce.

That night, a dozen or so girls were climbing onstage. I looked at twelve-year-old Moira and asked, "Do you want to go up?"

She was in.

It was a bit of a climb since the platform was in the way. As I was trying to give her a boost, I looked at the security guard and silently asked for his help. Without hesitation, he pitched in and the next thing we knew, Moira was running towards the rapidly forming crowd. In seconds, my daughter, with about a dozen of her new friends, was dancing with Bruce Springsteen!

I could not believe what I was seeing. Neither could the people around us. A woman we'd talked to prior to the concert was cheering and yelled to me with her thick Jersey accent, "Your daw-ta got onstage!"

As the song wound to a close, she walked over to Jake Clemons to tell him how much she'd loved his uncle and was enjoying his performance. Giant Jake bent down to listen to Moira, who was just shy of five feet tall, and put his fist to his heart, then flashed her the peace sign. It was a moment she will cherish forever.

On our way out of the venue, we saw another lucky fan from the night: the little boy who had gotten to sing with Bruce on "Waiting on a Sunny Day." His dad had also brought him, and as they headed for their car, he said, "I bet you're excited to tell your friends about this."

The boy shook his head. "I mean, I'll tell them, but they won't really understand."

Moira gave me a knowing look. Although over the years, she would introduce many of her friends to the band, she felt the same way.

I would obviously tell the story about my daughter getting on stage with Bruce and the E Street band as often as possible. I was excited to tell it to a group of fellow teachers and fans of Rock and Roll while taking part in the Rock and Roll Hall of Fame Summer Institute. This was a weeklong professional development I was fortunate to be part of, joining fellow students not only from Ohio but many from throughout the United States and even international.

I remember telling the story to a fellow Bruce and the band fan in the group from Australia. Bernie, this Australian Bruce fan, said right away, "Was it for 'Sunny Day,' mate?" This was not the last time this assumption would be made, but my focus was on having a conversation with someone from across the globe right in northeast Ohio, at the Rock and Roll Hall of Fame and we are discussing my daughter and the boss!

While we knew we could never duplicate getting onstage, we also know we are part of E Street Nation, and in this fervent fan base, if they are anywhere near your town, you go. So in February 2016, we would do just that.

We saw them on *The River* tour, celebrating one of the most iconic albums. Technically the plan for the concert was to play the complete album in order, but there's no such thing as a traditional E Street Band concert. They did pay tribute to the tour's namesake album, including some of my favorites, from "Sherry Darling" and "Out in the Street" to "The Ties That Bind" and, of course, "The River," but the band could never just stop at one album. Their set list also included classics like "Prove It All Night," "The Rising," "Thunder Road," "Growin' Up," "Born to Run," and a song about home, "Youngstown." Nils Lofgren rocked the house with a guitar solo for the ages during a song that spoke to us about our working-class town.

We loved the three-hour-plus show and decided we needed to go again when they came to Pittsburgh's arena, which has gone by many names, but at the time was Consol Energy Center. We got our tickets through Stevie Van Zandt's Rock and Roll Forever Foundation, which I love as an educator and will elaborate on later since he serves as our letter V.

This also gave us the chance to meet Stevie. He was just as nice as we'd hoped, thanking all the teachers in the room for their work, and we got a great photo with him. We also got to know some of our fellow fans in the room. One was there that night for her fiftieth concert!

Afterward, we heard a rumor that Nils Lofgren was right outside. So we took a walk and there he was. He talked with Moira and signed an autograph for her. We were so happy to see that Nils and Stevie are not only awesome as guitarists, but also extremely kind and accommodating to their fans. The concert had not even begun, and we were having a night to remember.

When the concert began, we instantly realized that although it was still technically the *River* tour, the band had abandoned the traditional set list. Perhaps it was because of the date.

It was September 11, 2016. Fifteen years to the day of the tragic terrorist attacks that would change our country forever. I remember picking Moira up from daycare on that day and looking at her, just one year old, knowing her generation would be growing up in a very different world than mine did.

No one taps into our culture like Bruce and the E Street Band. They opened with a string section-backed "New York City Serenade," followed by "Into the Fire," "My City in Ruins," and a speech from the lead singer that could only be described as a Preacher Bruce Moment.

They then kicked up the tempo and rocked "Darkness on the Edge of Town," "It's Hard to Be a Saint in the City," "Because the Night" and many more over the hours. One of my favorites was "Light of Day." It's a great song from a great movie that featured Armstrong family favorites Michael J. Fox and Joan Jett, plus this performance featured regional music legend Joe Grushecky of Joe Grushecky and the House Rockers!

Of course, Bruce isn't just about energetic concerts—although they are always exciting. We love Bruce because he speaks to us. His music is part of the fabric of places like my lifelong home in Northeast Ohio's Mahoning Valley. Even his newer albums reflect our lives. I keep the *Wrecking Ball* CD (yes, I still have CDs) in my car because it helps me deal with what I see at work every day: students and families impacted by the closing of the General Motors assembly plant in Lordstown. Our Valley is full of survivors, but songs like "Death to My Hometown" and "Wrecking Ball" speak to me as we face this latest challenge.

And as Moira's gone to college and made friends from out of state, Bruce's music has been the easiest way to explain the culture and atmosphere of where she's from. The Mahoning Valley is an interesting place with its political and labor history and people who aren't from around here have a hard time understanding what that's like. Bruce's music provides a pretty easy summary and some great tunes too.

We have tried to share how much Bruce and the band mean to us as much as possible over the years. We submitted a video to a documentary film called *Springsteen and I,* and while we were not chosen, we saw the film in Columbus and it was full of stories like ours (and is available on YouTube if you want to watch).

I also had the opportunity to host a show called *Be the Boss* on Sirius Radio's E Street station. Fans can select five songs and discuss why those particular numbers mean something to them. I had wanted to do it with my dad, but he was gone before we could make it happen. But soon after, I was able to participate.

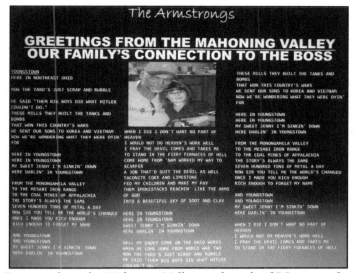

Greetings from the Mahoning Valley, in the style of "Greetings from Asbury Park," created for the Springsteen and I *video (Moira and her grandpa Ken in their Cleveland Browns wear)*

I first played "Youngstown" to honor my dad. He was a steel worker in Youngstown (as were my two grandfathers), where he started working in 1972 at 17 years old, and worked there until he was diagnosed with cancer.

Next up was "Factory," because I am one of many 2nd generation Bruce fans who was introduced to the Boss by their parents. My dad gave me all of his vinyl Bruce albums, something I cherish to this day. Now I have had the opportunity to introduce my daughter to the Boss. Her first experience with Bruce was the holiday classic "Santa Claus is Coming to Town," which I played next, followed by her favorite song (at the time) "Waiting on a Sunny Day."

I then told the story of my first Springsteen concert and finished my turn as the Boss on E Street Radio with one last song dedicated to my dad and his brothers. Dad worked with his brother Frank for over 30 years in the steel mill. They worked together, drove to work together, watched Cleveland Browns games together, fished together, and were what brothers should be. He and Uncle Frank and his oldest brother Dave were the best of friends. "Blood Brothers" was the perfect song to memorialize and honor them, as well as his sister Alma.

All of us have bucket lists and to Be the Boss on E Street Radio was on mine. Being able to talk about Moira and honor my dad on E Street Radio made it as perfect as it could be. Of course, it was nearly impossible to pick five, as it is for anyone asked to choose their favorites from their top band. My favorite changes by the week, day, or even hour. But no matter the song, the working-class lyrics, in-your-face guitar riffs, protest-laden fiddle solos, powerful sax solos, and overall energy speaks to me, my family, and everyone in the Valley.

Wrecking Ball included another song that spoke directly to me but this time a more personal rather than working class issue... though, as is common with Bruce, there is a connection. Bruce has talked openly in recent years about episodes of depression he has suffered from and discussed the inclusion of the song "This Depression" on the *Wrecking Ball* album.

Depression touches nearly all families and often just knowing other families are going through such issues can help one deal and overcome the struggles it brings. My family was greatly impacted by this. My mom struggled with depression as well as addiction throughout her life. As I have shared, she was only fourteen when I was born and I often thought her having us so young was why she behaved the way she did.

She was a caring person who would have months and years of good and stable times in her life but then there were periods in which it was obvious to me only later that she was suffering from depression. We lost her when she took her own life at age forty-nine. I thought about it a lot when I turned fifty thinking about the fact she never made it to fifty years. Could I have done something to change things? What if she had not had us so young?

I know from talking with others about their experiences, gaining knowledge about the topic through formal education and hearing authentic stories (and in song) from people like Bruce Springsteen, that no one is to blame for the mental illness our loved ones suffer. Recalling the good times and fun memories of those we lost from this disease is what can help us. Oftentimes that is through music.

We hope to see Bruce Springsteen and the E Street Band at least one more time before they, dare I say, retire. But retirement or not, the E Street Band will always fill our house and my car with the music of our lives. (And I do hope when we do get to see them, that they play "E Street Shuffle" or I will be forever in trouble with Moira.)

—Terry

OUTTAKES

The Eagles
July 2013 at Quicken Loans Arena in Cleveland, Ohio

We were not sure whether to put this in or not as Moira did not attend this with us. We did purchase three tickets to this concert with plans of her going but she ended up on her own adventure when the Eagles visited. I did feel bad that she did not get to see them, especially when we lost Glenn Frey. Moira and I did get to see Joe Walsh as a solo act and my hopes are high that they will tour as a group again. Maybe they will get Jackson Browne to do Glenn Frey's part—we heard a legendary story at their concert about how they lived one floor apart from each other in an apartment complex. They were fantastic that night in Cleveland as my friend Rob joined Kim and I, since Moira was out recording an album.

Every time this concert comes up and I say "we saw the Eagles!" Moira counters with "I recorded an album!" She was lucky enough that summer to attend the Stamps Baxter School of Music in Tennessee, a Southern Gospel music school led by some of the finest performers in the genre, and every year the group choir records a few selections for a CD. She and her grandparents all piled onto the stage with the conductor and the amazing pianist Tracy for a whirlwind few hours of recording. Moira still talks about this experience with such passion. We know she will never forget this amazing memory with her grandparents and now she has the literal album to remind her.

-Terry

Fleetwood Mac

February 18, 2015 at Quicken Loans Arena in Cleveland, Ohio

Fleetwood Mac was one of the bands my parents would listen to all the time on their turntable. Like many of a generation, they and I knew all songs of the *Rumours* album from beginning to end. The album is one of the more perfect complete albums ever recorded, achieving number one seller and one of the most critically acclaimed albums of all time.

Finances did not allow my mom or dad to see Fleetwood Mac live as they toured to support *Rumours* and later albums. In fact, I still recall talking music with my dad when I was young and him telling me that he saw REO Speedwagon (a band I would be introduced to and loved and would later see with Moira) but that was the only band of note he had seen live. He and Mom would go out and see cover bands at local bars, but they rarely saw major bands that had achieved commercial success, though later my mom did see a couple bands of note. The first was very memorable as my sister Jennifer won tickets on local radio to see George Michael. She and Mom went and loved it. I recall her later seeing Michael Bolton too. Obviously, Mom's tastes changed over time from the traditional classic rock while mine and my dad's preferences remained, well, classic.

Though my dad enjoyed the REO Speedwagon concert, the only acts he put on the same level as Fleetwood Mac were Bruce Springsteen and Janis Joplin. I was excited on his 50th Birthday when my Uncle and I took him out to see a local band that Kim, Moira, and I often enjoy, Guys without Ties. They had a female lead singer at the time who covered who else but Janis Joplin...and she was awesome. I later got him tickets for a stage show paying homage to Janis Joplin in Cleveland. He had great taste in music and I still think of him every time I hear Fleetwood Mac.

Terry with his Dad, Mom, and sister Jennifer

I loved sharing these stories with Kim and Moira. Kim was a fan of Stevie Nicks and Moira was hooked from the moment I shared the music video for "Tusk" with her. She was in her school's marching band and always hoped that they might play it one day.

Moira's third-grade teacher, with whom she remains friends, saw the band when she was young. She's told Moira many times, "When I saw Stevie Nicks standing up there on the stage, with all her scarves and her long coat swirling around her, I wanted to be her so badly."

We thought that we had missed our chance at an experience like this because the band had been on hiatus for so long. So, we were thrilled when the band reunited for a tour in 2015. It was incredible to see Lindsey, Christie, Mick, and Stevie up there side by side. They sounded to me just as they did on that vinyl many years ago. We sang along to all of the Fleetwood Mac hits, from the rocking opener "The Chain" to the second encore, featuring a rousing rendition of "Songbird." They even played "Tusk," accompanied by the music video behind them on a massive screen.

One of the most enchanting moments was the performance of

"Landslide." Moira and I believe that this is one of the most perfect songs ever recorded, and hearing it live from those who performed it was special, to say the least.

There was just one tiny glitch that night.

Following several years of teaching social studies, I was hired as the superintendent of schools for a district near my hometown. It just so happened it was also the first place I had taught, having been hired there six years earlier. However, in northeast Ohio, the duties of a superintendent also include determining whether to call off school due to weather, because freezing temperatures and lake effect snow are very common.

In our county, we have a system where superintendents consult each other to make this important decision, called the Weatherbird Network with the head of each group nicknamed "the Big Bird." I made the mistake of telling Kim and Moira about it and they have made fun of the name ever since. They've even threatened to buy a Big Bird from *Sesame Street* ornament for the tree if I become the "Big Bird." I would prefer something like "the Falcon," or even the nickname that one of my younger students gave me—"Jack Frost"—but I digress.

That night, the forecast called for both deep snow and cold temperatures. I decided it would be safest to cancel school the next day. But I knew I couldn't make the call with Stevie Nicks singing in the background. So, I made the call around 5 pm before we left for Cleveland, guaranteeing that I could make the call and ensuring that parents could arrange for childcare.

Many, many students replied to our district's tweet thanking me for the day off, but a parent at a basketball game the next night told me that she disagreed with the decision. It just goes to show what it can be like to serve as superintendent. I was glad to hear from another parent who appreciated the early notice, and since I knew her very well, I told her the story of the night before. "I decided to make the call early because I was worried you wouldn't be able to hear me over Stevie Nicks!"

Thick snow was starting to fall as we left the venue. We made it home safely, talking about our favorite moments of the night all the way back to Warren.

—Terry

OUTTAKES

John Fogerty
July 2015 at Jacobs Pavilion Nautica Stage in Cleveland, Ohio

Credence Clearwater Revival is a multi-generational family favorite for sure. Seeing Credence Clearwater Revisited resulted in a great time (twice) and we knew actually hearing John Fogerty belt out the classics would not disappoint. Far from it. He was fantastic. Jacobs Pavilion is on the small side too so it was one of those nights where it felt like he was performing just for us and a few friends. As a baseball fan, hearing John Fogerty perform "Centerfield" live was a checkmark off the bucket list to be sure.

We did see a few friends we knew at the Fogerty concert including Andy Gray, the entertainment writer for our hometown newspaper, *The Tribune Chronicle*. Gray's appropriately titled column *Gray Areas* has kept us up to date for years with local, regional and national acts coming through, their new music as well as making sure us locals know what is going on in the local performing arts scene. (As a mid-sized city we are fortunate to still have a quality newspaper and more than lucky to have a quality entertainment writer like Andy Gray. We look forward each week to an entire entertainment section titled *The Ticket*.)

After a twenty-plus song setlist that we did not want to see end we took a memory home with Moira grabbing a "Spread the Fogerty Vibes" t-shirt.   *-Terry*

Foghat
July 2014 at Ohio State Fairgrounds in Columbus, Ohio

"Fool for the City" and "Slow Ride" rocked the house as Foghat joined the triple bill with Bachman Turner Overdrive and Blue Oyster Cult at the State Fairgrounds in Columbus. We love this venue as they have brought many classic rockers to us with this concert being one of the first ones we saw there. Just like BTO and Blue Oyster Cult, Foghat was able to bring this classic rock crowd to their feet all night. *-Terry*

Foreigner
July 2017 at the Giant Center in Hershey, Pennsylvania

We love the music of Foreigner—who doesn't? I mean "Jukebox Hero" kind of says it all about Rock and Roll. Admittedly, the band is not even close to the original line-up, with only Mick Jones making an occasional appearance, but this did not stop us from enjoying hearing those memorable songs. While we enjoyed all the hits we also enjoyed hearing those around us as one of the older rockers in our area kept talking about the song "Starrider," hoping they would play it. When they did the look on his face was a great sight. All of us nearby cheered him on as they played his favorite song. That is something about music and concerts when it is a shared experience you instantly become a community with those you do not even know. *-Terry*

Aretha Franklin
July 2014 at Ohio State Fairgrounds in Columbus, Ohio

They don't call Aretha Franklin the Queen of Soul for nothing. Even in her 70s, her smooth, soaring voice filled the whole arena. We, like the rest of the crowd in Columbus, knew we were seeing an icon that night. Though this was on the trip where we came down with the Columbus Crud (see B for Beach Boys) and we could barely get to our feet to cheer, we had an absolutely incredible time. She was simply amazing! We are so thankful we saw her a few years before the world lost her in 2018. She is a legend! *-Moira*

GREEN DAY

April 18, 2015 at Public Hall in Cleveland, Ohio

*Moira at Cleveland Public Hall ready for inductions
that included Green Day*

As a lifelong rock fan and student of the genre, I was extremely lucky to have grown up only an hour away from the Rock and Roll Hall of Fame.

In the 1980s, the Hall of Fame Foundation considered many cities for the honor of housing the museum itself. New Orleans, Memphis, Chicago, San Francisco, New York. Everyone has an important connection to the history of rock and roll, but the city where Alan Freed coined the term "rock and roll" prevailed. In part because of fervent Ohioans who were encouraged to vote by the best radio station in the nation (100.7, WMMS Cleveland – Home

47

of the Buzzard), as well as civic leaders like George Voinovich and Mike White, and influential rock deejays such as Norm Nite, the Rock Hall would take its rightful place on the shores of the North Coast.

Architect I.M. Pei designed the physical building. When hired for the job, he told museum representatives that he didn't really know anything about rock, so they took him to concerts until he did. I read once that he believed "rock and roll is all about energy." That's more than reflected in the glass pyramid on the shores of Lake Erie.

I'll never forget the first time I visited. Every time I turned a corner, I saw something new: a pair of ZZ Top drums that had beards identical to those of the band members. A dress from gospel superstar and early influence Mahalia Jackson. A handwritten draft of the lyrics to Billy Joel's "My Life," in which the lyrics "got a call from an old friend, we used to be real close" are crossed out, even though if you listen to the song today, those are the lyrics that you'll hear. The top two floors feature rotating exhibits; during my first visit, it focused on Bruce Springsteen. But my absolute favorite of all time was "Louder Than Words," all about the inter-connections between rock music and politics. We even followed it to the Newseum in Washington DC. It was at the Louder than

Moira at Louder Than Words Exhibit

Words exhibit we felt the impact of Tom Morello of Rage Against the Machine. He came up again and again throughout this exhibit and his music and activism would be something we would see time and time again when rock meets causes.

I eventually was able to visit the archives, a massive library of books about rock music history and inductees, as well as papers donated by important figures. This sparked my dream of becoming a music librarian or a museum curator, and made several of the employees laugh, telling me, "I can't believe you know you want this career. Most of us are failed musicians."

We even decided to become members because we visited so often. This gave us the opportunity to bring friends, family, and visitors from out-of-town to the museum. We had the tour down to a science, sharing stories we learned from previous visits, from inductees we'd seen in concert, and from Rock Hall employees. It's one of my all-time favorite things to do with loved ones. And we've been mistaken for employees ourselves over the years—my dad's Rock Hall polo definitely contributes but so does the fact that I essentially act as a tour guide whenever I'm showing around someone new!

Being members provided us another benefit: we had first crack at tickets to the Rock and Roll Hall of Fame induction ceremony. At first, it rotated between Los Angeles, New York, and Cleveland. Eventually, Cleveland began hosting every other year.

We'd gone before to the simulcast in Cleveland, a livestream of the ceremony that was currently happening in New York. Cat Stevens, performing "Peace Train" with a huge gospel choir as a backup band. Joan Jett singing "Smells Like Teen Spirit" to honor Nirvana. My dad always tells me he never got Nirvana but that his brother Jason was a big fan...but he got it that night!

So in 2015, when the inductions were in Cleveland, we bought tickets. The slate of inductees was stellar: Lou Reed, Green Day, Stevie Ray Vaughn and Double Trouble, Joan Jett and the Blackhearts, Bill Withers, the Paul Butterfield Blues Band, and early influence the 5 Royales. And receiving the Award for Musical Excellence was Ringo Starr. It turned into an unmatched experience. I could see a concert every night and nothing would ever top it.

Faced with a lull in the action, Ringo and Paul McCartney started-ed acting the part of hosts; they told funny stories and interacted with the audience as stagehands moved equipment for the next performance. We would never have the chance to actually see the Beatles perform, but this was the closest thing there is left—and it was insanely cool.

Joan Jett's eyes welled up with tears as Public Hall gave her a standing ovation, and I found myself ready to cry, too. She performed three of her biggest hits—"Bad Reputation," "Cherry Bomb," and "Crimson and Clover"—joined by three additional legends. Our hometown favorite Warren, Ohio-born Dave Grohl, original Crimson and Clover artist Tommy James, and Miley Cyrus, who provided the induction speech, all joined in.

Joan is one of my all-time favorites. I had been wearing a t-shirt from one of her concerts to the Rock Hall every time we visited, in the hopes that maybe the employees or the building itself would pick up on the hint. I'd just never imagined that I'd get to watch it happen.

Bill Withers was heartwarming and hilarious, opening his speech with the line "I'm up way past my bedtime." He teamed up with Stevie Wonder, who gave the induction speech, to perform. Wonder commented that he wished he'd written songs like "Ain't No Sunshine" and "Lean on Me." He opened the latter with the wrong chords and started over, commenting, "Oops. I wasn't looking at the music."

Patti Smith gave a touching tribute to Lou Reed, ending with a spoken-word recitation of "Perfect Day." Stevie Ray Vaughn's brother Jimmy revealed the man behind the music while John Mayer gave our favorite induction speech of the night. It was clear how much he admired the late musician's guitar technique and the fiery emotion behind it. The Paul Butterfield Blues Band, with other stars like Peter Wolf sitting in, put an often-forgotten early form of rock in the spotlight.

And then Green Day—the subject of this chapter—took the stage. I must be honest, I had my doubts. Throughout the week of festivities, I had seen Green Day fans everywhere. They'd traveled, some of them thousands of miles, to see their induction or even just stake out the red carpet in the hopes of catching a glimpse of the band. I had a few close friends who were fervent fans, too, and clearly Fall Out Boy (who gave the induction speech) agreed. While I was only marginally familiar with the band, I didn't really get it. Then they started performing.

They roared through "American Idiot," which with a little research afterward, I discovered was one of the greatest protest songs ever written. They then moved right onto "When I Come Around." On the first time through the chorus, the band dropped out on the last line, and it seemed like all of Public Hall bellowed "when I come around" back at them. They ended with "Basket Case," and as the last chord died away, I realized: I got it.

During Ringo Starr's introduction, there had been a video tribute/compilation, with other famous drummers who had been influenced talking about this former Beatle. Green Day drummer Tre Cool spoke during the video, about how influential Ringo had been to his career and how much of a hero Ringo was to him.

The night concluded with the ultimate all-star rendition of "With A Little Help From my Friends." Everyone from throughout the night—Miley Cyrus, Green Day, Patti Smith, Bill Withers, Stevie Wonder, Joan Jett, Dave Grohl, John Legend, Karen O, Joe Walsh, Zac Brown, and of course the Beatles themselves. But no one was quite as memorable as Tre Cool, who, as the all-star band transitioned into "I Wanna Be Your Man," was playing on a second drum set next to Ringo himself. The look on his face was complete shock and awe.

It reminded me of something Billie Joe Armstrong said earlier, as he stepped up to the podium to accept his induction trophy: "My childhood record collection is in this room." And it was true. In addition to the legendary group onstage, we'd seen people like Yoko Ono and Jerry Lee Lewis in the audience. It was a dream come true for any rock fan. And though we attended induction ceremonies after that one, it was never topped. I don't think it ever will be.

It was pushing one in the morning by the time we left. We'd been there for over twelve hours. But as we walked out of Public Hall, our eardrums ringing, I would've gladly gone back in for twelve more.

—Moira

Moira with State Senator Capri Cafaro
at the Rock Hall inductions which included Green Day

OUTTAKES

Glass Harp
May 2016 at the Kent Stage in Kent, Ohio

This band formed in the Youngstown area and though they did not have a great deal of commercial success, they have a strong and committed following. The trio of Ohio natives (Phil Keaggy, John Sferra, and Daniel Pecchio) played Kent and other venues in Northeast Ohio going back to the '60s and '70s. Seeing them live in Kent where they were a staple for so many years just seemed so right. Their music had a unique sound and the guitar play was right up there with the best we have experienced. There is an urban legend of sorts that has Jimi Hendrix stating that Glass Harp's Phil Keaggy is the best up-and-coming guitarist on the music scene.

-Terry

HUEY LEWIS AND THE NEWS

July 14, 2015 at Packard Music Hall in Warren, Ohio

*Moira with Broadway actor (and all around awesome person)
John Dossett who starred in a jukebox musical featuring
the music of Huey Lewis and the News*

When I was twelve, I got my very first job. I was working at a car wash in my hometown. I thought this was cool at the time because not only was I making my own money, but I could listen to Y-103 and WSRD out of Youngstown and of course WMMS out of Cleveland for hours after school on weekdays and all day long on Saturdays and Sundays. The band I remember hearing more than any other was Huey Lewis and the News. "Do You Believe in Love," "Heart and Soul," and of course "The Power of Love" made the time fly as we shined up those whitewall tires and chrome.

Now, every time I hear the band, I think about my first job. I also remember that when MTV made it big, they were playing a lot of Huey Lewis and the News. Gen Xers my age will tell you how great it was to have music coming out of the television and seeing our musical heroes perform. You often hear bands talk about how they benefited from MTV and the exposure it gave them...I would contend that we fans benefited just as much.

Working at a young age did come with a price. I was never a great athlete but was decent in baseball in Warren's youth leagues. While I (all 5 foot 4 of me) tried out for our junior high basketball team (West Junior High School in Warren) and made it (surprisingly), it proved to me that either I had some athletic talent or the coach just thought I worked hard. I am still not 100% certain of which, though perhaps it says something that I can recall my coach yelling to other players "Shoot it, Brent!" and "Shoot it, Alfie!" but then yelling to me "Pass it, Armstrong!"

Regardless, the allure of having some money in my pocket at that young age was more important at the time. Thinking back, I likely spent much too much of my teenage years working. But as parents, Kim and I decided early on having one child and if we were blessed with good careers that we would not push our child to work during high school. That was important to me, to give her the time and freedom to explore clubs and activities. Moira ended up being active in Girl Scouts, Interact Club, and National Honor Society, as well as band. On top of that, she was quite an accomplished Speech and Debate competitor.

Back in the day, the Huey Lewis music I heard those many hours at the car wash quickly gave way to him becoming synonymous with *Back to the Future*. In my book, that only increased his credibility. He was a huge part of my teenage years and I would've loved to have seen him in concert. But the car wash didn't pay enough for tickets and this was before I was old enough to have a driver's license.

However, that dream came true for me later in life. In 2015, Huey Lewis and the News came to our hometown of Warren, Ohio, to the Packard Music Hall, and Moira, Kim, and I went. As he stepped out onto the stage, I remember thinking, "Does this man never age?" He had to be about twenty years older than me, but he looked just like he did when he graced the screen of MTV in the 1980s.

They played each one of their huge volume of hits as our

hometown crowd rocked. We also saw tons of people we knew in the audience. It seemed that everyone in the Mahoning Valley had been waiting for Huey and the News to come to Packard for about thirty years! It was a great night seeing my girls and many others enjoy a band we all considered legends. For that night, Warren was the heart of rock and roll!

As a family, one of our favorite topics of conversation is the concerts we've attended. There's often a follow-up story or a "post script." For example, a few years after we saw Joan Jett, she was inducted into the Rock Hall. Whenever we tell others that story, we recount how special it was seeing one of our favorite artists finally get her well-deserved induction. And when Huey Lewis comes up, it's accompanied by one of our favorite post scripts of all time and one of the most unique.

Moira is also a big fan of theatre and has been ever since she discovered the musical *Newsies* in middle school. She loved it so much that we traveled to New York City to see it on Broadway. Moira was so excited to be with her fellow fans, affectionately known as Fansies, and we got to the theatre early.

While we were waiting to go in, Moira noticed actor John Dossett on his way into the theatre. He played publisher Joseph Pulitzer in the show. She knew who he was immediately. I was not as up on my Broadway stars, but I instantly noticed that he had a Steelers hat on. I'm a Browns fan and harbor some resentment towards the Steelers because our hometown is about dead center between Cleveland and Pittsburgh, and I grew up listening to Steelers fans brag about their Super Bowls and abuse my Browns.

So as Moira stopped him for a picture, I joked, "This is the first time I let my daughter get a picture with anyone in a Steelers hat!"

He laughed, posed for the picture, and headed into the theatre.

But then he turned back around and walked back to us.

"What are you folks doing after the show?" he asked.

"We just have to catch a bus back to Ohio around eleven," I answered.

"Would you like to come backstage?"

After I picked Moira up off the ground, we of course accepted the invitation. Standing on the stage of a Broadway theatre was an amazing experience and I will never forget the look on Moira's face as John showed us around the backstage area, pointed out different props from the show, and introduced us to other members of the cast.

We stayed in touch with John as we returned to see *Newsies* several times before its closing in 2014. Afterwards, we returned to New York City to see his other shows like *War Paint*; we also have traveled to some regional theatres in the US to see him perform. We soon found out that he is not just the talented Tony-nominated actor that we saw onstage but also a wonderful person.

You're likely asking yourself, "What does this have to do with Huey Lewis and the News?" Good question! Well, John was a part of the cast of a jukebox musical featuring the music of Huey Lewis and the News called *The Heart of Rock and Roll*. The show premiered in San Diego in 2019.

It's the story of a Chicago musician named Bobby who can't take the life of a musician anymore, so he trades in his guitar for a corporate job. After falling in love with his boss, Cassandra, he gets a final shot at stardom and she gets a chance to become CEO. They have to decide which they value more: love or their jobs. John played Cassandra's father, the founder of the business.

We recently went to see him in a play and afterwards talked to him about his experience with the show. He told us that Mr. Lewis was often at the theatre to support the cast and was a very genuine, nice guy. We hope that this show makes it to Broadway in the future so we can celebrate both John and the music of the News.

—Terry

OUTTAKES

Happy Together Tour
September 2015 at the Canfield Fairgrounds inCanfield, Ohio

The Happy Together Tour comes near us every year with a collection of rock legends. September 2015 version featured Flo and Eddie of the Turtles ("Happy Together"), The Association ("Windy," "Along comes Mary"), The Buckinghams ("Kind of a Drag"), The Grassroots ("Temptation Eyes"), the Cowsills (*Hair*: "Let the Sunshine In"), and Mark Lindsay (Paul Revere and the Raiders lead singer). It is not often you can see so many memorable songs by classic groups in one place but this was it.

Moira brought a friend with her as we made it to yet another Ohio county fair to see the Happy Together Tour. This was not just some everyday county fair though...this was the iconic Canfield Fair in our neighboring county of Mahoning (we live in Trumbull County). The largest county fair in Ohio and one of the largest in the country that often has dictated school calendars. Check it out if you find yourself in Northeast Ohio any Labor Day weekend. As the rooster in their advertising says, It's something to crow about!

-Terry

Heart
July 2014 at the Ohio State Fairground in Columbus Ohio
July 2016 at Riverbend Music Center in Cincinnati, Ohio

We love the concert series at the Ohio State Fairgrounds for many reasons we have shared throughout the book. One reason is the awesome acts in such a short span of time and it less than three hours away from home. In July of 2014 we saw the Beach Boys (with John Stamos), Queen of Soul Aretha Franklin, Joan Jett and the Blackhearts and Heart, all in the span of three days. From "Barracuda" to "What About Love," the Wilson sisters reminded us of just how many songs we knew *by Heart*.   *-Terry*

BILLY IDOL

August 7, 2019 at DTE Energy Center in Clarkston, Michigan

Moira at American Bandstand exhibit located at Rock and Roll Hall of Fame. The exhibit's video features Billy Idol and many more!

In the depths of the Rock Hall, after you navigate through the catacombs of costumes and push through the constant crowds in the Beatles and Stones display, there's a little theater off to the side. It's just before you pass into *Right Here Right Now*. Most people ignore it. Unless they're with me. I won't let them.

It's the *American Bandstand* video, which plays on a loop and highlights some of the best moments in the show's 50-year history: Cyndi Lauper tells Dick Clark that she smuggled chocolates from England for him, the Bangles thank him profusely for allowing

58

them to perform on the show before they made it big, he refers to Gladys Knight and the Pips as Gladys Pips and the Knights on three separate occasions. There are dozens of little moments that my dad and I, who have watched the whole thing countless times, recall and talk about. Billy Idol's segment is one of our favorites.

After a clip of "White Wedding," Dick Clark mentions that Billy once lived in London and now lives in New York. He then asks, "New York is very similar to London, is it not?" Billy agrees. "They're focused cities. You know what's going on. That's how I met these people, that's why we're making this music."

The segment immediately after features Bryan Adams, who sings a bit of "Straight from the Heart" before learning the proper pronunciation of "New Yawk," where his drummer is from, from the host.

Between that experience and my general love for their music, I'd wanted to see both performers for a very long time. I had skipped seeing Bryan Adams in high school because I had a paper due. Although I'm pretty sure I got an A on the paper, I later really regretted missing the concert. And in 2012, Billy Idol played the week before Joan Jett at ArtPark and everyone at her concert had t-shirts from his. And we're big fans of the movie *The Wedding Singer*, where Billy listens to the distraught main character's story of heartbreak and sympathizes, leading to the iconic line "Billy Idol gets it." When they went on tour together, it seemed like the perfect opportunity.

The plan was by no means complete, though. I spent my fall semester of freshman year studying in Italy and my dad came to visit and travel with me. There, on a plane from Rome, Italy, to Geneva, Switzerland, we ate an entire Milka Oreo bar and watched a John Mulaney comedy special for the first time. People were staring because we couldn't stop laughing but we didn't care. We *loved* John Mulaney and quoted him constantly, especially his bit about college, substituting my university's downfalls: "I gave you more money than the Civil War cost and you can't give me fresh fruit in the dining hall?" When he announced a performance at the Comedy Hall of Fame, we decided we had to go. The Comedy Hall of Fame is located in Lucille Ball's hometown of Jamestown, New York…a short two hour drive from our home in Warren so why not right?

But then a quirky favorite musical of mine called *Be More Chill* announced its final performance.

So we added a stop.

Then George Takei, an activist hero of mine, announced an appearance at Steel City Con near Pittsburgh (only an hour and half from home).

So we did some rearranging.

Then my best friend Ani announced that he was moving to Michigan.

One more adjustment.

Finally, we landed on a visit to Michigan for the concert and one last visit with Ani. Then, to the John Mulaney show in upstate New York. Then back across the state of Pennsylvania to Steel City Con. After that, off to the airport and a flight to New York for the closing performance of *Be More Chill.*

Moira with Ani

About a month before the trip, I went out to lunch with my friend Grace. We talked summer plans—for her, marching band, and for me, this massive trip. I excitedly explained all the details, and she looked across the table at me and said, "I have a headache now."

I couldn't blame her. It was chaotic, it was a little crazy. And for us, it was completely normal. We've almost never visited only one place on vacation; the summer after my senior year, we visited Disney World, Fort Lauderdale, Savannah, Cape Cod, and Boston all in a two-week rush. All in the car of course. No better way to see the local flavors. And we're certainly not strangers to last-minute plans—I remember very vividly that January night in 2012 that my dad got the call from our Congressman Tim Ryan. The Congressman would later run for the Democratic nomination for President and previously helped my dad get tickets for his students to the 2009 presidential inauguration and would again in 2016. Apparently, his office had extra tickets to that Monday's inauguration of President Obama in 2012—less than 4 days away. Of course, we packed our bags and went. This was not unusual for us.

In August, we again packed our bags and took off for a whirlwind weekend. The drive to Michigan was mostly smooth sailing, a welcome break from an unlucky string of storms we'd been hitting lately, until we approached Clarkston itself. There was massive construction along the route, and we were lucky that we left early because

Moira with Congressman Ryan

we spent a while sitting in gridlock. But we made it to the venue on time.

I hadn't been to DTE Energy Center since the Beach Boys concert in 2011 and was surprised to find that it looked familiar to me. But really, all outdoor venues like that—from Blossom near our hometown to Riverbend in Cincinnati to DTE—look fairly similar.

As we took our seats, we didn't have to wait long. At three minutes to seven, the lights dimmed and Billy Idol's backing band took the stage. We were shocked—rock usually runs on its own time, a little behind everything else—and felt terrible for all the people who were still stuck in traffic, leaving whole rows bare.

But Billy didn't seem to mind. He swept onstage in a long patchwork coat reminiscent of Steven Tyler, and immediately launched into "Dancing with Myself." He didn't look like he aged a day since that performance on American Bandstand, even as he shed several layers and ended up shirtless.

His band rocked right along with him. I think we were in the minority, not knowing their names before that night—so many people burst into cheers as they took the stage, leaving me wondering whether Billy Idol had changed his look that dramatically since

I'd last seen him. But soon I was shouting right along with them as the guitarist and bassist played powerful solos, often accompanied by Billy standing next to them playing air guitar.

He played all of our favorites, stopping frequently to chug blue Gatorade and pumping his fist in the air to punctuate his lyrics. And he did something I hadn't seen in over one hundred previous concerts: he stopped in the middle of songs to sign autographs for the dozens of audience members close to the stage who held up albums and posters.

He even played a throwback from his punk days: "Your Generation," which he said was about the fourth song he wrote. Though I generally stick to classic rock, I love how punk resonates with every generation; the lyrics were meaningful to me, and my parents hadn't even met when he was with Generation X in 1977.

The applause for his cries of "How you doing, Michigan?" weren't as strong as some hometown crowds manage, and I soon realized that we weren't the only Ohioans who made the trip—I noticed several Cleveland sports jerseys and a sign in front of us that read "Ohio loves you!" I had to agree.

But by far, the best moment of the night was when he stood center stage and told us all a story.

"A few years ago, I was recording a new album called *Kings and Queens of the Underground*. We recorded it in London and I went to visit my parents to play them the album, because my mom always wanted to hear what I was up to. My dad was never really into my music, but he loved this album, and while we talked, he even started asking me about the punk band I was in, Generation X, and what our songs meant." He paused, a little emotional. "Unfortunately, my dad got cancer. Five years ago to this day he died. I wasn't able to be there, but my mom told me that he was listening to *Kings and Queens of the Underground*, and this song was playing when he died."

He then played a charged rendition of "Ghosts in my Guitar." I watched the screen

Terry's Take

During the pandemic I took up walking in our local park for exercise, closing in on 50 and all, and often listened to "Ghost in my Guitar" as it made me think of that concert, that trip, and my daughter away at college.

behind him flash through old photos of him with his dad—ending with a modern one, this punk rocker in leather onstage holding hands with his dad, who was in khakis and a dress shirt.

My dad squeezed my hand. I looked over at him, feeling a little choked up, and he smiled.

"Billy Idol gets it," he whispered.

As he closed his set, he thanked all of us for making his life "so effing great" and then thanked his incredible guitarist, Steve, for the same reason. Then he exclaimed, "Steve, show them what a hit looks like!" and they launched into "White Wedding."

That wasn't the last we'd see of him that night. He returned for a number with Bryan Adams (whose performance was also fantastic, and who also doesn't age—the Fountain of Youth must be hidden somewhere in the back room of a record company). Since Bryan followed Billy in the *American Bandstand* lineup, they'd become forever grouped together in my mind. But as I watched them play together, Bryan Adams on his knees riffing on his guitar and Billy wailing into a mike, both grinning widely, it seemed that they were friends in real life, too. Nothing could've made me happier.

The rest of our road trip lived up to the standard set by that first night. Ani and I explored his new hometown with the windows down and the cast albums to *Hadestown* and *Hamilton* blasting. We laughed so hard we cried at John Mulaney's jokes. And I cried pretty hard at *Be More Chill*'s final stage door as I said goodbye to a show I love.

A few days after we came home, I went to lunch with Grace again. I was about to move back to college and she wanted to say goodbye, plus get an update on the rest of my summer. As we slid into a booth at our favorite restaurant, she asked, "How was that monster trip you had planned?"

I talked for about twenty minutes, recounting some of my favorite moments and memories, and could've kept going, but she held up a hand to stop me. "Moira," she said. "While I'm definitely enjoying this, you haven't even made it past the concert yet, and I'm afraid you won't get to tell me about New York City before you have to go back to Kent!"

—*Moira*

OUTTAKES

Donnie Iris
May 2016 at the Warren Community Amphitheater in Warren, Ohio

In many regions throughout the country, you can find local musicians so popular and well known that their concert attendance and audience support will rival any nationally famous rock legends. Donnie Iris is one of them. Kim and I actually saw him and his band the Cruisers in the '90s but their history goes back much further than that. They had national hits, partly due to getting play on MTV, with "Ah Leah" and "Love is Like a Rock" in the early '80s. Hailing from Pittsburgh, PA they had a huge following in Pennsylvania as well as Northeast Ohio towns like Cleveland and Youngstown and many of the towns in between.

I was very excited when I saw they were going to play the Warren Community Amphitheater in our hometown. The amphitheater itself is home to a series of tribute bands each summer that draw sellout crowds. It has been part of a rebirth of sorts for our downtown area of Warren, along with new restaurants and shops. Though I saw Donnie Iris in Cleveland with some friends (along with a drunk lady who yelled "Welcome to Cleveland, Donnie!" about 100 times during the show) I have seen a few concerts here myself but it was a special moment seeing Donnie Iris with my daughter right in our hometown. *-Terry*

Moira with friends at the Rock Hall

JOAN JETT

June 11, 2013 at ArtPark in Buffalo, New York

July 30, 2014 at the Ohio State Fair in Columbus, Ohio

April 18, 2015 at Public Hall in Cleveland, Ohio (Rock Hall inductions)

May 15, 2015 at Nationwide Arena in Columbus, Ohio

July 22, 2016 at the Riverbend Music Center in Cincinnati, Ohio

June 27, 2018 at Blue Hills Bank Pavilion in Boston, Massachusetts

July 7, 2019 at Progressive Field in Cleveland, Ohio (All Star weekend)

Moira with the awesome Joan Jett!

I saw Joan Jett for the first time in 2013 and my life changed.

Before that night, I had heard the big hits: "I Love Rock and Roll." "Bad Reputation." "Crimson and Clover." But that night, she threw open the doors to her entire music history. I heard "Cherry Bomb," "Androgynous," and even a preview of her upcoming album *Unvarnished*, which features songs like "Soulmates to Strangers," "Any Weather," and "Everybody Needs a Hero" that remain some of my favorites to this day.

After the concert ended, we drove up to Niagara Falls, not far from the concert venue in Buffalo. As I stared into the water, I could almost still hear the lyrics echoing in my ears. I wanted to be Joan Jett, this strong woman who didn't let anybody stop her and doesn't care what anybody thinks of her.

From then on, she became a staple of my music. There was a song for anything I was going through, and I kept a notebook full of favorite lyrics that inspired me. And I wrote letter after letter to the Rock and Roll Hall of Fame, begging for her induction, even insisting on wearing a t-shirt from one of her concerts every time we visited.

In 2015, I got my wish, and I got to be there for the ceremony. As Public Hall gave her a standing ovation, I saw tears in her eyes. Suddenly, I was crying too. Miley Cyrus, who delivered her induction speech, called her the most deserving person for induction. Clearly, everyone in Public Hall thought so, too.

In my wildest dreams, I never thought I'd see that in person. And in my wildest dreams, I never imagined that I would someday get to actually meet her in person. But those "beyond my wildest dreams" moments kept happening.

The second, however, wasn't a completely happy moment.

In 2016, I got sick. My body reacted very badly to a medication called Bactrim that I was taking for a sinus infection and I was diagnosed with an extremely rare condition called Stevens Johnson Syndrome (SJS), which causes lesions on skin and mucus membranes. That's the technical definition. When you're experiencing it, it's excruciating pain, exhaustion, and overwhelming fear, because a disease you've never even heard of is tearing your body apart.

It's still taking a toll on my body, but I did recover. I'm very lucky that I had a doctor who recognized the symptoms early on and that I lived close to Akron Children's Hospital, whose brilliant doctors helped me recover (and brought dozens of medical students to see me so that they would recognize cases in the future). It wasn't easy, though. I missed weeks of school, fell asleep on the couch after doing simple things like showering, and pretty much lived on Ensure protein drinks. And music.

SJS can be fatal and just knowing that—even when the danger has passed—is terrifying. I coped through speech and debate, where original oratory let me explore how our society treats mortality, and lots of reading and writing (this is where my passion for John Donne sprouted, which consistently confuses my English professors, for whom getting students to read his work is usually like pulling teeth). There was also always music. Background noise for my reading and writing, sometimes, but also proof that I wasn't alone. Other people had felt this way before and put it into lyrics and melodies that were right there at my fingertips to help me heal.

Terry's Take

My friend Mark was working at the concert venue and told me one of their responsibilities was to support on-site talent and Joan Jett was one of them. He shared with me that a younger person working for them referred to her as Jett Joan. Times like that I am even more thankful for Moira as a twenty year old with awesome music taste.

A lot of it was the music of Joan Jett. Her songs perfectly expressed how I was feeling: that desire to feel strong again, that knowledge that life is fleeting, and sometimes just unbridled joy. Because there were undoubtedly those moments, too, like when my speech about mortality propelled me to the state semifinals.

The summer after, when I was mostly healthy again, we bought tickets to one of her concerts. I was thrilled. I already knew how much fun her concerts were, but now it would be even more meaningful.

Meanwhile, my dad, unbeknownst to me, wrote to Joan Jett's manager, Kenny Laguna and told him my story. Dad told him we were going to see Joan in Cincinnati. Mr. Laguna wrote to my dad giving him instructions on what to do when we arrive:

1. *Go to will call*
2. *Tell them your name and that Kenny Laguna left two passes for us*

3. *Go to a location to the right of the stage and tell the "guard" who you are and show them the pass to meet up with Joan's tour manager*

Dad told me what was going on once we went to will call. We followed Mr. Laguna's instructions to a tee. I was already beyond excited for that night. It was a triple bill of Joan, Cheap Trick (another favorite), and Heart. As Cheap Trick started their set, we met her tour manager and the others who were meeting her that day behind the stage and he walked us back to a tent. He announced that she didn't have much time and wouldn't be signing autographs but would be happy to take pictures and talk to us.

I was shaking by the time we reached the front of the line. Her manager walked me up to her and said, "Joan, this is Moira, the girl who was in the children's hospital."

Someone had clearly told her about me, because she nodded and immediately pulled me into a hug.

"I'm so glad you're here," she whispered. I started crying and she squeezed me tighter. "We're going to have a great time tonight."

I don't remember all the details of what she said and I don't know how long I stood there in her arms, but I do remember that every time I thought she'd let go, she didn't. And even though she technically wasn't signing autographs that night, she signed a pair of my black Converse tennis shoes for me. It was the first pair I ever owned. A pair that I had bought in 2013 after seeing her in concert for the first time and noticed her entire band wearing them.

Moira's Joan Jett-signed Chuck Taylors

On the left, she wrote "Moira—rock those toes!" and on the other, "Dance hard!" She gave me and my dad each one last hug and a smile, and we headed to our seats. Cheap Trick was just reaching the chorus of "Dream Police."

I talked about that moment for months. There are so many stereotypes about how rock stars are, and horror stories about people who meet their heroes only to discover that they're nothing like they imagined. I had the opposite. She had exceeded my expectations.

Two years later, I qualified for the national speech and debate tournament in Fort Lauderdale. We drove down from Ohio, stopping in Orlando and Savannah along the way. Then, we drove up to Massachusetts to see our friend John (John Dossett from the Huey Lewis chapter) in a play on Cape Cod and spend a day in Boston I told one of my friends about the plan, referring to the stopover in Massachusetts—on the way from Florida to Ohio—a "side trip"; he looked at me and said, "Moira, that's not a side trip. That's its own trip!"

Nonetheless, we drove the extra few hours and after a day of following the Freedom Trail throughout Boston, my dad had a surprise for me: we were heading to a concert that night. It was a triple bill of Tesla, Foreigner, and Joan Jett. I had the opportunity to meet her again! He was usually so bad at keeping secrets, I was amazed he kept it quiet for that morning.

I was proud of myself for not bursting into tears this time, but Joan was as sweet as ever. I told her how much meeting her had meant to me and thanked her for taking the time to talk to me not just then, but today, too. She smiled at me and said, "Of course. That's what rock and roll is all about."

And she's absolutely right. That is what rock and roll is all about. It's just like she said in her induction speech: "I come from a place where rock and roll means something. It means more than music, more than fashion, more than a good pose...it's a subculture of integrity, rebellion, frustration, alienation, and the glue that set several generations free of unnatural social and self-suppression."

That's what Joan did for me when I first heard her music coming from a car radio. When I was becoming a teenager, when I was sick, when I was going to college, when I was facing the hardest points in my life, Joan's music continued to make me realize that I didn't have to be anyone other than myself. I could speak up for what I believed in. I could love rock and roll and it would carry me through.

I've seen Joan perform almost every year since that first concert in 2013. I love it more and more every single time. The latest was this year at the All-Star Game festivities in Cleveland; she provided a great end to a day that included the Celebrity Softball Game and All-Star Futures Game. Like a superstitious baseball player, she even jumped over the first base line when leaving the stage in the infield. This excited my dad very much.

I was a bit disappointed that the crowd had not shown as much passion as a regular Joan crowd as she sang "Bad Reputation" and "I Love Rock and Roll." My dad and I made up for them.

But maybe I'm just a little biased. I can't thank Joan and the Blackhearts, and Kenny Laguna enough for their kindness and inspiration.

—*Moira*

Moira meets Rock & Roll heroine Joan Jett for the first time

OUTTAKES

J. Geils Band
December 2014 at Quicken Loans Arena in Cleveland, Ohio

A common beef people have with the Rock and Roll Hall of Fame is why one band is in and another, perhaps equally talented and equally successful, is not? I try to wait patiently for my favorites to get in, while Moira tends to write letters—like why Joan Jett should be in—until they get it. They added an exhibit that allows fans to choose a band to be nominated. Sure, there are many deserving bands still not in, but I vote for the same one every time: the J. Geils Band!

Peter Wolf, often confused with the name J. Geils due to being lead singer of the band, is a great frontman. We saw them open for Bob Seegar. I love Bob Seegar but this night in Cleveland he was co-headlining. The live rendition of "Musta Got Lost" is forever etched in my mind from that night at the Q.   -*Terry*

Billy Joel
February 2014 at Consol Energy Center in Pittsburgh, Pennsylvania
January 2020 at Madison Square Garden in New York, New York

Growing up, I heard legendary stories about the time Elton John and Billy Joel toured together. It seemed that everyone in the Mahoning Valley was there—except me, of course. I hadn't been born yet. But loving both the Rocket Man and the Piano Man, I was so glad to eventually get to see them both. And when Billy Joel pulled out his harmonica to start that iconic song, the audience went wild—only for him to laugh, saying, "You don't know what I'm going to play yet!"

My Dad would tell me how many times he used to listen to Billy Joel's album *The Nylon Curtain*. Once I listened to the songs I could see why he loved that album which includes the catchy "Pressure;" "Allentown," which is a page right out of the Mahoning Valley where we live; and the emotion-filled and brotherly "Goodnight Saigon." We rocked the night away, reminding ourselves of a time we were pulling into our local grocery store and the quick drum solo of "Still Rock and Roll to Me" was on. As we were stopped, we took the chance to do some air drumming and happened to look over at a lady in another car. She just gave us the biggest smile...Billy Joel would be proud!

I also had a cool assignment in one of my middle school language arts classes that split us into groups and then assigned each group a verse from "We Didn't Start The Fire." We had to research the historical context and describe why each word or phrase was included. I loved that class and it was one of my favorite assignments from all of my years of schooling.

My dad and I have made our share of trips to New York City due to my love of Broadway and the city that never sleeps in general. In early 2020, I had the opportunity to attend a theater fan celebration known as BroadwayCon. I had been lucky enough to attend the first one five years earlier but this time I was there to cover it for an online theater magazine I write for called Curtain Call.

While there my dad checked out other activities we could see and was excited to find that Billy Joel would be playing at Madison Square Garden. Seeing an event at Madison Square Garden was on my dad's bucket list, but seeing Billy Joel in New York City brought it to a whole new level.

My dad often refers to Madison Square Garden when remembering days spent watching Pro Wrestling on television with his grandparents. He'd share stories about Bruno Sammartino and Larry Zbyszko and other wrestlers from previous eras that graced the ring at as he says announcer Gorilla Monsoon would describe MSG as "The Mecca of Pro Wrestling." He even saw some of their memorabilia amongst the many artifacts inside MSG.

Seeing Billy Joel in this venue was amazing. The crowd was exactly as you would expect at a NYC Billy Joel concert and we knew quickly that many in the crowd had seen him several times during his MSG residency. He played all the great hits and mixed in some New York favorites and even had a big surprise in store for us as well.

Halfway through the set he introduced a friend to join him in a few songs. That friend was Jon Bon Jovi! The crowd, including us, went crazy and rocked right along with the Piano Man from New York and his friend from New Jersey. *-Moira*

Elton John
April 2013 at the Nutter Center in Dayton, Ohio
March 2016 at the Covelli Center in Youngstown, Ohio

The first time I saw Elton John was my 13th Birthday. I brought a sign with me that said "Celebrating my 13th Birthday with Elton John." He came over to my side of the stage, waved at me and mouthed "Happy Birthday!" It was so exciting. When "Crocodile Rock" came on, my dad started making motions with his hands like a Crocodile's mouth. I told him "Dad, that's not a thing." Next thing I know people around us started to do the same. Okay... perhaps it became a thing.

It's good that I had this concert as a memory of Elton, because the second time I saw him was just a few days before I was hospitalized with SJS. Thankfully I had great memories from that first show to fall back on. We were also thrilled when *Rocketman* came out and we saw the story of his life onscreen. He is a true showman and one of our family's all-time favorites.   *-Moira*

Journey
August 2013 at the Illinois State Fair in Springfield, Illinois
June 2016 at Blossom Music Center in Cuyahoga Falls, Ohio

The first time we saw Journey, on a double bill with Night Ranger, the show was tremendous. We had to leave early in their set though as Moira was not feeling well. Not having heard our favorite songs, including of course "Don't Stop Believing," we returned to Blossom a few years later and tied up the loose end. Arnel Pineda proved to be what everyone would tell us as he carried the ball for Steve Perry. The band made sure we won't stop believin' in Journey.   *-Terry*

Kim's Commentary

From being with Terry since High School he knew I liked Steve Perry so he would always make the comment "He looks like he needs a bath" (No offense Mr. Perry) Of course, I always had a retort: "Jealous."

73

KISS

**August 26, 2014 at Blossom Music Center
in Cuyahoga Falls, Ohio (with Def Leppard)**

March 17, 2019 at Quicken Loans Arena in Cleveland, Ohio

*Terry (as Ace) and his sister Jen (Paul Stanley)
on Halloween as kids circa 1979*

When I was a kid, I loved the band KISS more than anything. I had all of their albums growing up and all of my friends listened to me constantly talk about my favorite songs. There was even one Halloween where my sister, two of my cousins, and I dressed up as the band and went trick-or-treating through all of our neighborhoods.

My grandpa knew about my love for the band, too. He heard me talk about how much I loved their music and admired their talent for marketing, even at an early age. He also enjoyed music. My sister and I spent many of our childhood weekends at he and my grandma's house. I remember many days when I went out to visit him where he was working in the garage. The radio would always be on in the background, providing a soundtrack of Elvis,

Johnny Cash, and more. For some reason I recall him enjoying Kim Carnes' "Bettie Davis Eyes" as he worked. I also recall him enjoying a particular local deejay. Even at a young age I picked up on the fact the fellow was trying to be the Mahoning Valley's version of Wolfman Jack.

Grandpa also humored me as I watched the TV movie *Kiss Meets the Phantom of the Park*. It was required viewing for all of us in the Kiss Army back then. We actually thought it was good television at the time. Watching it now, and reading about everything that occurred behind the scenes, I cringe. But my grandpa was right there alongside me as I obsessed over my absolute favorite band in the world at the time.

In the late 1970s, he decided he wanted to take me to a KISS concert. Our local Sears store had what was then called Ticketron. It was inside our local brick-and-mortar Sears store. On the morning that tickets went on sale for that particular concert, he drove out to the store and stood in the long line of die-hard fans, some of whom had been there all night.

By the time he reached the front, the performance was completely sold out. He never told me this story and we lost him much too young, but after he passed, my grandma told me the story. He was a truly great man who I continue to admire to this day. That story always makes me grateful that I had someone in my life who was so supportive of everything I loved.

As I grew up, I continued to follow the band's career. I also advocated for their induction into the Rock and Roll Hall of Fame. I never went as far as some fans, who boycotted the Rock Hall until they got in. They did finally get their due in 2014, to my delight. And to Moira's, as she was then able to take a friend to the Rock Hall whose father had sworn off going until KISS got in!

That same year, I finally got to live my dream and fulfill my grandpa's quest that day from the 1970s. I also got to take my daughter with me! It was a sweltering August day and we were seeing the concert at the outdoor Blossom Music Center.

We almost always have bad luck with the weather when we try to attend concerts at Blossom. A few years back, we invited Kim's parents, sister Donna, and brother-in-law Norman to Blossom to see the Cleveland Orchestra play a night of Disney music. While we don't all share a taste for rock music, we are all fans of all things Disney. We thought this we be a great way to enjoy a concert with the whole family. What we didn't count on was rain.

The concert wasn't cancelled and we weren't going to cancel either. Thankfully, when we pulled into the parking lot, Kim's parents announced that they had ponchos in their trunk that would help keep the rain off everyone. We were so glad that we could still enjoy the concert without getting wet. So they started handing out the ponchos. I got a blue one, Moira got a red one, everyone had plain colored ponchos...until they got to Kim. She ended up with a camouflage poncho.

Despite having grown up in the country, Kim is a city person now and not a camo wearer at all, so of all people to end up with that poncho, it was hilarious that it ended up with her. We still laugh about it and have adopted the nickname Camo Kim into the family lexicon. She now also sports a deer sticker on the back of her car—placed there by her dad who was carrying on the joke, but she decided to keep it there.

Blossom as the venue is the only similarity to that Disney concert. You couldn't get any more different from a double bill of not only KISS, but also another hard rock band, Def Leppard. The crowd went wild and had a chance to warm up their singing voices as they played many of their iconic tunes, including "Pour Some Sugar On Me." As they repeated the chorus, they stopped playing, allowing just the sound of the roaring crowd's voices to sing the chorus for them.

And then Gene Simmons, Paul Stanley, Tommy Thayer and Eric Singer took the stage. I had been dreaming of this moment since I was that kid watching *The Phantom of the Park*. They did not disappoint. They performed just as you would expect; the image of Gene Simmons breathing fire across the stage is branded in my mind forever. It was amazing to see them as late as they are into their careers, performing with the same energy they had when they began.

I was able to see them one more time, this time without Moira. (Although we generally don't count those, she's fine with me attending if she has seen the band before.) It was in 2019 on what they claimed was their farewell tour. I was just glad that I had the chance to see them blast the audience again with thunderous renditions of their classic hits. I was officially, passionately, re-enlisted in the KISS Army, just like I was when I was a kid.

—*Terry*

Terry's grandfather, Paul Hess, when he was in the army.
Paul stood in line for hours in hopes of getting Terry tickets to see KISS

OUTTAKES

Kansas
August 2012 at the Ohio State Fairgrounds in Columbus, Ohio

Kansas was co-headlining a state fairground show in Columbus. "Carry On Wayward Son" and "Dust in the Wind" were songs I and most everyone my age had heard many times, becoming part of our personal music history. I did get to see them another time with a friend. Moira's rule was that I could only go see a band with some-one else if we have already seen them together first. This "Wayward Son" carried on both times seeing that band from Kansas! -*Terry*

CYNDI LAUPER

November 2, 2013 at Quicken Loans Arena in Cleveland, Ohio
(part of Scott Hamilton Ice Skating benefit)

May 2, 2014 at Quicken Loans Arena
in Cleveland, Ohio (with Cher)

The Armstrong family meets Rowdy Roddy Piper
and can't help but talk about who else: Cyndi Lauper

My dad is terrible at keeping secrets.

I can't blame him. It's not like he means to spoil the surprises. He just gets excited about whatever gifts he has hidden away for the next holiday and can't help telling us about it. Like when he got my mom tickets to a Cher concert for Mother's Day. He told me that we were going, but we'd tucked the tickets inside my mom's card and hadn't told her yet.

Then, one day, we were all sitting in the living room together and he looked up from his phone to say, "Wow, Cyndi Lauper is the opening act when we go to see Cher!"

"We're going to see Cher?" my mom exclaimed.

Dad looked furious with himself. I started laughing.

I knew exactly why he was so excited about this one. We had seen Cyndi Lauper before—and were completely disappointed. Not with Cyndi herself. She played a great set of all our favorites. It wasn't the show itself, either. She was singing accompaniment to an ice-skating show put on by legendary skater Scott Hamilton to benefit the Cleveland Clinic. It was different, and cool, to see routines set to some of our favorite music. My mom loved figure skating, too—she's told me many stories from when she and my dad first started dating, when she would go to wrestling shows and political talks for him and he would go to Sea World and figure skating shows with her.

The crowd was the problem. "Girls Just Wanna Have Fun" is one of the most iconic songs in music history. Everyone should at least know the words to the chorus, or at least pick up on it, since it's repeated often and also the title of the song. But, no—we were seated right next to a section of what looked to be high-dollar donors. Though we could appreciate their contributions to the cause, they didn't appear to know a single word. In fact, they seemed downright bored. Even Cyndi picked up on it, slowly drifting away from our side of the stage as the song progressed and soon stating, "How are my people up there?" gesturing to the upper seating.

"I read online that there's an after party, where the big donors get to meet her," my mom said as we walked back to the car at the end of the night. "I can't imagine that—Cyndi Lauper, with those dry people who didn't even know her most famous song."

Thankfully, the audience at the Cher concert was nothing like that. Though Cyndi was the opening act, they treated her like the superstar she is. And when a big group in the front walked in late, she called them out with a roll of her eyes: "Welcome to the show. Eff you."

She again played all of her hits, but this time, we weren't the only ones singing along. She also surprised us with an acoustic rendition of "Not My Father's Son," from the show *Kinky Boots*. *Kinky*

Boots is one of my favorite Broadway shows and had run since my first visit to New York City. We had walked by the Al Hirschfield Theater that housed the musical during every visit we would make to New York. Cyndi had written the music and lyrics, even winning a Tony Award for her score. This number is one of the most emotionally impactful songs from the show and there were tears in my eyes as she played this version.

She even talked about how much she liked Cleveland. Since we often get thrown under the umbrella of flyover country or associated just with our losing sports teams or burning river, I was glad to hear that someone appreciates Cleveland for its charms. And the Rock Hall, of course. Although she did have one criticism. "Induct more women!" she admonished.

She's right, of course. She's one of the many, many deserving female performers, songwriters, and behind-the-scenes forces who deserve induction.

In my freshman year of college, I took a history of rock class; my roommate at the time, after watching me skim the textbook, informed me that I probably could've taught the course, but I loved it anyway. We spent a week talking about the genre's women, all the way back to blues divas like Ruth Brown. While Motown girl groups broke through, their images, music, and careers were constructed and run by men, and my awesome professor pointed out that even stars like Janis Joplin have a hidden moral of the story: we remember her because of her death, and associate that with the message that girls can't be rockers.

Thanks in part to the women's movement, that all started to change. MTV also played a huge role, allowing finally women to define themselves. Cyndi was one of the pioneers with songs that spoke to every facet of this revolutionary movement, and with videos that exemplified how MTV could be used for profit and expression.

Rock has always had this aspect of running right alongside social movements. In that class, we also talked about how minorities—people of color, the LGBTQ+ community, women, and dissenters of all types—have found their voices in music. And how music has provided solace and protest for the hardest times in our history—a particularly touching message considering just a few steps away was the hill where four students were shot while protesting the Vietnam War, sparking the Crosby Stills Nash and Young song "Ohio."

That class will stick with me forever. Especially one afternoon, as late winter was starting to turn to spring, and the sun was setting, filling the room with a warm light. Dr. Bindas paused his lecture, looked around at us, and said, "It's you, the young people. It's always been you changing the world."

I blamed it on the fact that Bob Dylan was playing in the background, since folk music is essentially emotional manipulation, but I was actually crying as I walked out of class that day.

That's one of the things I love about this genre of music. History and rock are invariably intertwined. Cyndi is one of the best examples and as she barreled through songs like "She Bop" and "Money Changes Everything," she proved that she also has legendary status just as a prolific performer.

Cher's portion of the concert was fantastic, too. She has a very different style than Cyndi. She changed outfits, or at least wigs, between every song. There were elaborate lighting shows, backup dancers, and huge props including a massive horse that she rode in on for a "Dark Lady"/"Gypsies Tramps and Thieves" medley. At one point, she sailed around Quicken Loans Arena in a glittering, gazebo-like structure.

It was a memorable night, to say the least, and one more image was branded permanently in my mind as we drove out of Cleveland. As we turned by Playhouse Square, a new addition was lighting up the block: the outdoor chandelier. After months of construction, it was unveiled and lit for the first time ever that night. It was a beautiful sight, shining and sparkling over Euclid Avenue. Five years later, and it's hard to remember what the theatre district looked like without it.

Shortly after, my mom and I went to a wrestling show with my dad. Most people are shocked to learn this, but he's a die-hard fan. His grandma used to take him to shows and genuinely believed that everything happening in the ring was legit, even occasionally throwing flash cubes at the bad guys! Dad was just as passionate, even doing a stint a few times as a ring announcer for a pro wrestler/ promoter he became friends with, Preston Steele, and living out an item on his bucket list: performing as a wrestling manager. He created a character known as Fabulous Freddy Foxx and managed the team of The Bouncer and Psycho Mike.

When Dad was principal, Preston Steele did a benefit show at his school, where my

Manager Terry (center) as Fabulous Freddy Foxx with Psycho Mike and the Bouncer

younger cousin Mallory instantly transformed into a shouting Grandma Hess incarnate. That, coupled with wrestler Doink the Clown dousing my other cousin Morgan with water during the show, made it a night to remember.

My dad's favorite wrestler of all time is "Rowdy" Roddy Piper. Uncle Roddy, as my dad refers to him, was—as I have heard my entire life—the most entertaining wrestler of his era. He transcended pro wrestling. My dad would say that without Roddy Piper there would have been nowhere near the success that Hulk Hogan and the WWF/WWE ended up achieving. Roddy had just the right timing and personality to get you to love or hate him...and fans would turn on a dime whenever he wanted them to.

In the 1980s professional wrestling went from a combination of territories to the beginning of the global empire that would become World Wrestling Entertainment. The vehicle used to make it mainstream was an ingenious idea called the "Rock N' Wrestling Connection." MTV was enlisted in this venture and matches like the "War to Settle the Score" and "The Brawl to End it All" were broadcast to a much larger and diverse audience. Cyndi Lauper took center stage in a feud that would include the involvement of Rowdy Roddy Piper. The heat between the two, and the other wrestlers involved in the feud, was made believable by Lauper and Piper's on-screen antics. You really believed they hated each other.

My dad had attended many wrestling shows before I was born, and had not gone in a while, but when he heard Uncle Roddy was going to be at a show down the road in Youngstown, he jumped on it. And when we had the chance to meet him, we grabbed it. I hadn't even been thinking when I threw on my Cyndi Lauper t-shirt that morning—I didn't have any wrestling merch, so I went with my default outfit: a concert tee. But when we finally reached the front of the line to meet Roddy, he zeroed in on my shirt.

"She has the best voice," he raved. "And she was great to work with."

I was now excited, too. Although not nearly as excited as my dad, who had Roddy sign his program from the first WrestleMania to which Roddy commented, "Wow! Not many of these still around." (Dad had attended a live showing of the very first Wrestlemania on closed circuit television at the Packard Music Hall).

My dad even got to tell Roddy about his grandma and how she introduced him to wrestling. Roddy was incredibly nice, asking him, "Is she still with us?" and taking a photo. I later learned that after my mom and I turned to go, Roddy shook my dad's hand and said, "You have a beautiful family."

The world lost Roddy Piper not long after we had the honor of meeting him. Whenever my dad talks about meeting him, he says "That was big-time" I hope his family knows the impact he made on other families that he touched during his career...even Cyndi Lauper fans!

Terry's Gramma Hess with wrestler Preston Steele

That is another aspect of rock that I adore: it can build connections between people who, on the surface, couldn't be more different. Like that night: from a professional wrestler...to Cyndi Lauper.

—*Moira*

OUTTAKES

Kenny Loggins
June 1985 at Blossom Music Center in Cuyahoga Falls, Ohio
(Terry's first concert)
August 2017 at the Lorain County Fair in Lorain, Ohio

Throughout high school, I don't know what I would've done without my friend Mason. He was vice president of my speech team, an officer in our Political Action Club, and my biggest supporter in and out of school. He also loved Kenny Loggins. So, my dad and I always kept an eye on his tour schedule, but he mostly stuck to the West Coast—until a date popped up at the 2017 Lorain County Fair. We immediately bought tickets and Mason and his dad joined me and mine for a fantastic night, despite the little bit of rain! We even ended up with guitar picks from a roadie. It was a great full-circle moment: from my dad's first concert with his friend so many years ago, and now he was able to take me and my friend. *-Moira*

Lynyrd Skynyrd
September 2015 at the Fulton County Fair in Wauseon, Ohio

Normally, we love traveling to see different bands, exploring new cities, and experiencing a variety of venues. For this concert we were in a more rural area, much like many county fairs. I remember walking past a stand selling t-shirts that said "I love my redneck boyfriend" with the companion t-shirt "I'm the redneck boyfriend." I pointed it out to my dad and asked, "Oh my gosh, who would actually buy that?" Then we turned the corner and saw a couple wearing them. To each their own, we agreed. Despite our feeling a bit out of place, Lynyrd Skynyrd would not leave us disappointed. Again…rock brings people of different cultures and backgrounds together! We had a great time as they played such classics as "Simple Man," "Sweet Home Alabama," and my dad's high school class song, "Freebird." *-Moira*

PAUL MCCARTNEY

August 18, 2016 at Quicken Loans Arena in Cleveland, Ohio

*Paul McCartney and his band waiving flags
(and toasting the crowd as well)*

Moira and Kim are quite the Anglophiles. Moira has UK blood, from both of us. Whether it is their love of tea (complete with a tea corner), the royals, or British rock, our home in Northeast Ohio could be transported to Jolly Ole England and we would not skip a beat. Even our weather, complete with cloud cover and misty rain, makes one think of a scene out of Londoners grabbing their bumbershoots.

The Beatles are one of those imports from England that we have always enjoyed as a family. So many iconic songs and one of the most historical groups in history. We have visited their exhibit at the Rock and Roll Hall of Fame many times, complete with suits that they wore, instruments they played, and merchandise that were sold to their legions of fans. This display, placed right next to the

Rolling Stones exhibit, is one we make sure to see on every trip to the Rock Hall. Prior to schools offering History of Rock and Roll classes, the Beatles was one of the few bands you could learn about in a history class.

We taught Moira early on about the Beatles being on Ed Sullivan and passed along stories about the response teenager girls had to them when they landed in America. One thing that always surprised me was the Beatles' working class roots in Liverpool. I had them stereotyped due to the suits they donned as the early Beatles from upper middle class of England.

All the stories we shared with Moira about the Beatles were re-inforced at the Rock and Roll Hall of Fame American Bandstand video. The video includes Dick Clark moderating a talk of several '50s-era teenage girls discussing the Beatles. When you make it to the Rock and Roll Hall of Fame in Cleveland, you must check it out!

As noted previously in this book, we have been fortunate to see the two living Beatles (see page 51 of G for Green Day, when Ringo Starr was inducted into the Rock and Roll Hall of Fame). When we heard Sir Paul was coming to Cleveland on his 2016 tour, we were able to snag three tickets for his second night at Quicken Loans Arena. Sadly, Kim was not able to go with us. Moira and I talked about who we could get to go in her place and Moira came up with the perfect person to take. One of her high school friends, Dante, was a Beatles fan and had never been to a concert. I knew him from he and Moira being on the Speech and Debate team together and he was always one of the nicest young men I could come across. He rocked along right with Moira and I and somehow, he had all of the rock concert mannerisms and cultural

Terry's Take

Writing about one of the Beatles I could not help but think of a group of my friends from high school and how we began a text group on weekends during the pandemic. We often talked about music and one night boy bands came up and a few were mocking them. This was right after we were all unanimously saying how much we loved the Beatles. Steve from our group reminded us: Guys you know the Beatles are a boy band.

norms down. Moira indeed had picked the perfect guest for the evening!

The night began with the Beatles classic "A Hard Day's Night" and "Can't Buy Me Love." Sir Paul and the band perfectly weaved in iconic Beatles songs and Wings classics "Live and Let Die," "Band on the Run," and my personal favorite Wings song, "Jet." We had not done much recon before coming to the concert and were shocked when they went for three hours and nearly forty songs! It had the feel of a Springsteen concert.

Prior to the encore, Paul McCartney and his bandmates would come out to interact with the crowd in the most spectacular way. Four of his band members came out with flags in hand waving them for all the crowd to see: the Ohio flag, the British flag, the American flag, and the gay pride flag. The crowd went crazy, including us, and Moira and I could not help but think we were seeing something new and cool. We also laughed when drummer Abe Laboriel did not have a flag but instead toasted everyone with a wide smile, glass of wine in hand.

We have been to Disney's Epcot a couple of times and always spend a great deal of time in England. We always make sure to see the current British Invasion cover band each time. We cannot wait until the current Covid-19 pandemic is over so we can head across the pond making stops at the numerous landmarks of the British Invasion, like walking in the steps of the Beatles strolling across that walkway captured on the Abbey Road album cover and taking in the other British rock sites and tours. When we finally make it across the pond, at the front of our minds will be the night in Cleveland seeing Sir Paul McCartney live.

—Terry

OUTTAKES

Yo Yo Ma
August 2010 at Blossom Music Center in Cuyahoga Falls, Ohio

We were so excited to take Moira to see Yo Yo Ma so early on in our concert going exploits. Though Yo Yo Ma is not Rock and Roll, he is not your boiler-late cellist either. His creativity and collaborations have given him staying power that most classical musicians seek. It was great to see his talent and genius was also matched by his kindness. He once visited our hometown of Warren, Ohio and had several local musicians sit in and play with him and during the Covid-19 pandemic he played to entertain those at his vaccination site. It bears pointing out that our love of Yo Yo Ma was perpetuated when he made a classic appearance on one of our favorite television shows, *The West Wing*. We often repeat the question and answer from the episode when Donna Moss (played by Janel Moloney) asks Josh Lyman (played by Bradley Whitford) about a Yo Yo Ma concert. "Was he good?" asks Moss, to which Lyman naturally replies, "He's Yo Yo Ma." Well said.   *-Terry*

Barry Manilow
March 2015 at the Wolstein Center in Cleveland, Ohio

When thinking of all of the venues at which we have seen concerts, I was excited to learn that our Barry Manilow concert would be at the Wolstein Center. The center is on the campus of Cleveland State University. We love CSU and it was on Moira's list of colleges, making it to the Elite Eight.

Kim, Moira and I loved the Barry Manilow concert. The Dave Koz Band was a fantastic opening act. Manilow led the crowd singing along to hits "Can't Smile Without You," "Mandy," and "Copacabana." What a great night with a legend on his One Last Night tour.   *-Terry*

Mannheim Steamroller
November 2009 at Quicken Loans Arena in Cleveland, Ohio

Yes, it's not exactly classic rock, but Mannheim Steamroller was my first concert. I was spellbound by their theatrical show and remember to this day how in awe I was, hearing songs come to life before my eyes. It sparked my passion for live music forever. As we drove home with my mom's family (Aunt Donna, Uncle Norman, Nan and Pa Pigott with me, my mom and dad) the snow was really coming down. At one point snow would enter the vehicle right onto my aunt. The holidays were officially under way!   *-Moira*

Kim's family. Front row: Uncle Norman, Aunt Donna, Moira, and Kim Back Row: Pa Pigott, Nan Pigott, and Terry

John Mellencamp
January 2015 at Playhouse Square in Cleveland, Ohio

To many of us, John Mellencamp is the Midwest Bruce Springsteen. His music finds a way to grab you like very few others can. From his early hits like "I Need a Lover" to MTV era "Jack and Diane" and "Hurts So Good," he finds a way to your heart and head waxing nostalgia throughout.

When we heard him that night in Cleveland, I could not help but think of a road trip to the former Geauga Lake Amusement park, about an hour from Warren that my friends and I took soon after graduation. We jammed in a van all the way home with "Jack and Diane," singing along as we closed in on the end to our senior year.

We were also lucky to have an exhibit of some of his art at our local museum, the Butler. It was a very cool exhibit that made some very powerful political statements, plus it was always cool to see what the interests and talents of musicians are offstage.

I had the *American Fool* album and remember borrowing my dad's *Scarecrow* cassette (did I make a copy of it?..nah). John Mellencamp made a mark on this midwestern family...now three generations worth! *-Terry*

Terry's Take

Like most groups of friends, we love sharing our useless knowledge with one another. My friend John, who was taking lead on our "Jack and Diane" singing (in the van on our Geauga Lake trip) is our go-to for music trivia. Though we all hold our own, John takes it to another level.

Moondog Coronation Ball
2012-2015 at Quicken Loans Arena, Cleveland, Ohio

In 1952, Cleveland's own Alan Freed, who is credited with coining the term "Rock and Roll," teamed up with local businesses to host the "Moondog Coronation Ball." Now widely accepted as the world's first rock and roll concert, it also ended in a manner typical of rock and roll: tickets were oversold, the authorities were worried about a riot, and the show was shut down after the opening act. Now, there's an annual tribute to that original event. We went four years in a row and have seen so many great throwback acts.

2012: Sam Moore of Sam and Dave, Mickey Dolenz of the Monkees, KC and the Sunshine Band, and Creedence Clearwater Revisited. Davy Jones had passed away just a few months beforehand, and there was a beautiful slideshow in tribute during "Daydream Believer." As we waited for Sam Moore the band played "Hold on, I'm Coming." Creedence Clearwater Revisited fronted by Bulldog rocked the house like no one else and my dad made sure to do what had become a tradition. If there was a band or song my mom really liked, and she was not at the concert, my dad would call our home phone and leave the live song on the answering machine.

That night it was nearly all of KC and the Sunshine Band's set.

2013: The Temptations, Three Dog Night, and the Doobie Brothers. This was chock-full of the best moments. The Temptations, lined up in sparkly green suits, dancing in unison. Three Dog Night explaining to us the origins of their name and playing their hits. My mom would exclaim "I love Three Dog Night!" and soon download all of their songs on her Ipod. The Doobie Brothers singing "Black Water," one of our favorite songs of all time, and ending with everyone on stage for "Listen to the Music."

2014: The Family Stone, Peter Noone of Herman's Hermits, Steppenwolf and Tommy James and the Shondells. We actually ended up meeting Peter Noone at intermission, when he was hanging out at the merch table, and snapped a picture. As my dad sent it to some of his friends, his iPhone insistently autocorrected the name to "Peter No One." The Family Stone rocked all of Sly and the Family Stone's hits, Steppenwolf brought the hard rock to the event with "Born to Be Wild" and "Magic Carpet Ride," and we were blown away by Tommy James.

2015: Smokey Robinson, BJ Thomas, Mark Lindsay, and Randy Bachman. We've always had a list of artists/bands we wanted to see, and Smokey Robinson was near the top of the list. We were very excited when it was announced that he would be headlining the Moondog Coronation Ball. When Smokey sang, he engaged the crowd at the top of his game. "Cruisin" and "Being with You" were so well done. BJ Thomas regaled the crowd with "Hooked on a Feeling" and "Raindrops Keep Falling on my Head." Mark Lindsey sang his Paul Revere and the Raider's favorites and Randy Bachman mixed in BTO classics we love and added some Guess Who classics like "American Woman." *-Moira*

INTERMISSION

Moira, Terry, and Kim –
Concerts By the Numbers

While you take a break from the concert action,
enjoy some fun facts from the Armstrongs...

Performers seen (unique; each counted once): 281

Performances seen (performers counted each time we saw): 420

Rock and Roller seen the most times: 7 (Joan Jett and the Blackhearts)

Number of different venues: 58

Closest venue to home: 10 miles
(numerous artists at Packard Music Hall)

Farthest venue from home: 2118 miles round-trip
(Air Supply at Disney Epcot Center in Orlando)

Total miles driven to venues (estimated): 27,001

Most frequently attended venues:
Packard Music Hall in Warren, Ohio: 27
Quicken Loans Arena in Cleveland, Ohio: 23
Playhouse Square in Cleveland, Ohio: 16

Hall of Fame Inductees Seen:
Rock and Roll Hall of Fame: 59
Country Music Hall of Fame: 3
Gospel Music Hall of Fame: 2
Southern Gospel Hall of Fame: 8
Rock Hall and Gospel Music Hall of Fame: 1 (Aretha Franklin)
Country Music, Gospel Music, and Southern Gospel
Halls of Fame: 1 (Dolly Parton)

Most expensive ticket: $400 for Bruce Springsteen
and the E Street Band (TeachRock Fundraiser)

Biggest bang for the buck: $5 for Joan Jett (2013 in Buffalo)

Favorite merch. items:
Moira (tie): Cheap Trick guitar picks, Chuck Taylors signed by Joan Jett
Terry: Drum sticks snagged from Styx show
Kim: Cyndi Lauper hoodie (Neil Diamond hoodie a close second)

NIGHT RANGER

August 18, 2013 at the Illinois State Fair in Springfield, Illinois

Our trek to see Night Ranger was the last leg of a summer 2013 trip that featured Moira and I attending "Elvis Week" in Memphis. Moira is a huge Elvis fan, as you may know from her writings in this book about the King of Rock and Roll. That part of the trip was awesome and even had a tie-in to seeing Night Ranger.

We were talking with a very nice family at an event that was part of Elvis Week when the typical "Where are you from?" "What do you do?" and "How did you become an Elvis fan?" questions come up. We mentioned that on our way home to Ohio, we would be stopping in Springfield, Illinois, to see Journey and Night Ranger at the Illinois State Fair.

The dad of the family got this huge smile, before explaining that Night Ranger was one of his favorite bands. As he looked to his wife and daughter, he quickly and excitedly reeled off the names Kelly Keagy, Jack Blades, and Brad Gillis, the musicians who have been the heart of the band for decades. Occasionally on our Rock and Roll journey we would run into a family with a child with them that, like Moira, actually looked like they wanted to be there. Obviously, this interaction got us even more excited about heading to see Night Ranger and Journey!

We had never seen Journey or Night Ranger, so this promised to be a great night. The concert was at the Illinois State Fairgrounds. We had seen many concerts at the Ohio State Fair in Columbus, so we thought how different could this be? We quickly found that we were not in Columbus anymore, Toto.

As we drove into town, we followed the signs directing us to the fairgrounds, but did not find "official" parking. Quickly we decided to park at one of those homes in close proximity to a popular venue (like a state fair down the street) who take their locale as an opportunity to hose their fellow man—or, to be more "FC" (fiscally correct), earn some extra income by selling parking spaces in front of their house.

When we got out of the car, it was obvious that we were not in the best part of town. As I was putting any items of value in the trunk, I told Moira that if there was something she really liked in the car, she should put it in her bag and take it in with her as the car could probably be gone when we get back. I was half-joking; I was sure it would work out okay. It was more of a lack of familiarity with the area and the belief that a family from Illinois headed to Columbus for a concert at the Ohio State Fair would feel the same sense of unease. But when traveling with your middle school daughter you have your guard up more than normal.

Graduating in 1989, Night Ranger's music was a standard, from "Sister Christian" at high school dances to the drive home from working at Sbarro Pizza jamming to "Don't Tell Me You Love Me." And of course the more obscure but to a fan of actor Michael J Fox the title song of *Secret of My Success!*

Moira and I arrived early enough to make our way to the front of the pit before Night Ranger took the stage. The weather was just ideal. While waiting for the action to start, we enjoyed the landscape dotted with ferris wheels and kiddy land rides as well as the smell of

Kim's Commentary

I think we watched *Secret of My Success* our first few dates. I was not sure if Terry kept forgetting we watched it, was it the only VCR tape he owned, or did he just want to keep listening to Night Ranger singing the title song?

fair food. They showed quickly why they have had the staying power they have, and the crowd responded with great passion, singing along to their classics.

The concerns I had parking the car spilled over into the concert itself. There were some in the crowd that were a bit on the rowdy side which was a bit surprising as this was Night Ranger and Journey in 2013, not the Rolling Stones in 1969. Somehow recalling the skills I picked up when I made that West Junior Basketball team in seventh grade, I was able to use my knowledge of boxing out. I surrounded Moira as she was in the front at the barrier to keep her safe. All was good.

While we enjoyed the music, there was some commotion back behind us. A fight had broken out. I concentrated on keeping Moira safe when, of all things, Night Ranger jumped into action. Jack Blades stopped singing and then stopped the rest of the band. He got everyone's attention, pointedly looking at the guys fighting and saying, "What's wrong with you? We're playing a ballad!" It was a classic way of disarming a potentially dangerous situation and the band went on to jam the rest of the night.

We loved Night Ranger and reminisce about this experience all the time. In hindsight, even the parking was not as bad as we first thought. We were just in a hurry and in unfamiliar territory. Night Ranger was still the band that Dad we met in Memphis with his family had excitedly talked about. Journey would come on next, leading the way with "Separate Ways," but we needed to get on the road. Eventually we would make up for it by seeing them another time...making this night about Night Ranger and how they can still Rock in America!

—Terry

OUTTAKES

National Quartet Conventions
2012 and 2013 at Leconte Center in Pigeon Forge, Tennessee

I inherited most of my music taste from my parents, but I'm also very close to my grandparents. Some of their favorites rubbed off as well. They loved southern gospel, a genre full of rollicking pianos and tight harmonies. I attended dozens of concerts with them, even singing our favorite songs at nursing homes and churches with them on occasion and going to Ben Speer's famous school of southern gospel. And for two years, we also went to the National Quartet Convention, a massive celebration of the genre with a huge exhibition hall, delicious ice cream, and moving multi-hour concerts every night. *-Moira*

Randy Newman
July 2015 at Heinz Hall in Pittsburgh, Pennsylvania

Since it's home to the Rock Hall, a few concert venues, the second largest theater district in the United States (Playhouse Square), and my dad's favorite sports teams, we spend a lot of time driving to Cleveland. I've also been introducing my favorite spots to friends for years, especially now that I'm in college and many of my friends are out-of-staters. And without fail, every time we drive into the city, we listen to Randy Newman's "Burn On Big River." (For the uninitiated if you have seen the baseball movie *Major League*, you can hear it at the beginning of the move). Since I clock in at five feet tall on a good day, I'm also pretty partial to "Short People." My dad loves the

Terry's Take

Newman's "Burn on Big River" is a reminder of the grittiness of living in Northeast Ohio. Leave it to Clevelanders to take a negative and turn it into a positive naming beers (Burning River Ale) and coffee (Burning River Coffee)

Toy Story movies, so he's a big fan of "You've Got a Friend in Me." Basically, Randy Newman is an old favorite. We saw him in concert—backed by a symphony orchestra!—and adored it. *-Moira*

THE O'JAYS

October 26, 2019 at Playhouse Square in Cleveland, Ohio

The O'Jays rock and connect to one of our family's greatest loves: books!

This book has already brought up many of our family passions. Things we love, like history and politics and feminism and so much more, are all interconnected to music. But we are also all readers. Some of my earliest childhood memories are of my parents reading out loud to me, from bedtime stories to just for fun. And it didn't just stop with the books. I remember going to meet Junie B. Jones, the protagonist of a book series I loved, when she went on a tour across the country. We went to meet authors, too, saw stage productions based on books we loved like *The Best Christmas Pageant Ever*, and even dove deep into the subjects of books. After reading *Charlie and the Chocolate Factory*, we saw the movie and toured a chocolate factory near our hometown.

I was also very lucky to have teachers throughout grade school that really valued books, too. My third-grade teacher, Mrs. Baer, who remains a friend of mine to this day, was probably the best. She had a background in theatre and read dozens of books out loud to us over the course of the school years, including several *Little House on the Prairie* books and the *Poppy and Rye* series by Avi. The next year, I was disappointed by my language arts class, when the teacher assigned us a novel that we could read at our own pace. I finished it as quickly as possible and snuck out of the classroom to sit outside the door of Mrs. Baer's classroom and listen to her reading out loud to her classes.

Moira with Mrs. Baer

Books are a deeply ingrained part of our family. Our tastes are all different—my dad sticks to nonfiction; my mom is a fan of cozy murder mysteries, fantasy, and sci-fi; and I'm more along the lines of historical and realistic fiction. But there are books we can all agree on, and we also try at all points to pass on our love of books to others. Every time someone in our lives has a baby, they receive a copy of *Moira's Birthday* (an incredible book by Robert Munsch, a family favorite author, and one of the only representations of my name that I could find outside of Peter Pan) and *The Polar Express*. (I once started crying during band in high school because nobody else in the class realized that it was a book before it was a movie.) Also, when my mom spoke on Career Day at my elementary school, she presented lesson plans based on a holiday favorite called *Auntie Claus*. When it became clear that the students weren't familiar with it, we bought copies and distributed them throughout the lower grades of the school district in the hopes that more students would be exposed to these books we love so much.

Now, our love of literature doesn't seem like something that will flow naturally into our love of music as easily as some of those other things we all love as a family. However, the *Toys Go Out* series was an exception.

These were some of my absolute favorite books when I was a kid. They're about a stuffed buffalo named Lumphy, a stuffed sting-ray named StingRay, and a red rubber ball named Plastic, along with all their friends, who have adventures while the little girl who owns them is away. In one of the books, Lumphy goes with the little girl on a picnic. It starts to rain, so the girl and her dad quickly pack everything into the picnic basket and dash back to the car. However, in their haste, they don't get the lid all the way on the jar of peanut butter. Lumphy is covered in peanut butter by the time they get home. The girl's dad says that Lumphy needs to be washed. Lumphy isn't worried at first, but then StingRay tells him about how terrifying the basement is, full of dust, spiders, and axe murderers. He's terrified and decides to hide in the closet. The girl searches for him for days and is heartbroken when she can't find him. When he hears her crying, he can't take it anymore. He comes out of hiding and the little girl, overjoyed, takes him downstairs to wash him so they can get back to playing.

He's still a little worried, because the basement is dark and dirty and he's a little intimidated, particularly when the dryer starts rumbling intimidatingly. However, then the washing machine speaks up. His name is Frank, and he's thrilled to have someone new to talk to. He explains to Lumphy how he works and as the spin cycle begins, he sings to help Lumphy through the fear and accompanying nausea. He makes up a song about a brave little buffalo and has a beautiful voice.

Later in the story, Lumphy brings the whole gang down from the little girl's room to have a party in the basement, and Frank provides the music, singing "Love Train" by the O'Jays. I actually wasn't familiar with the song, but I looked it up and loved it, and immediately began fantasizing that every time I could hear the gurgling of our own washing machine from the basement, that it was Frank singing out that classic Motown number to the delight of all of my own stuffed animals—the ranks of which included a stuffed buffalo, stingray, and rubber ball in honor of the book series, of course.

I had the opportunity to meet the author of this influential series, Emily Jenkins, at a wonderful program in my town called English Festival. It involved reading a set of about ten books and then meeting at a local university for related activities. Some of Emily's young adult novels, written under the name E. Lockhart, were on the reading list one year when I was in high school. While doing some preliminary research, I discovered that this was the same author as *Toys Go Out*. I decided that instead of asking her to sign my copies of the books at the meet and greet session, I was going to bring my StingRay, which had been made for me by my grandma when she couldn't find one to buy, and ask Emily to sign it.

I'm not usually one to get starstruck, but I absolutely was as we reached the front of the line. However, as soon as I started telling my story and pulled my StingRay out of my backpack, a huge smile broke across Emily's face and I was put at ease. She loved it. It remains one of my all-time favorite author-related memories.

A few years later, during my sophomore year of college, I was texting my dad about plans for an upcoming weekend. My roommate Jordan and I were coming to my hometown to judge a speech and debate tournament and I was commenting that we would probably head back to Kent that night afterwards and hang out there with our friend Kit.

My dad replied, "Can I ask a favor? The O'Jays are at Playhouse Square. I would love to have them in the book. We could drop Jordan off at Kent if that helps, or she can come, or we could pick up a group to come for that matter...whatever it takes."

I immediately agreed, as did Jordan and Kit. When I responded that we were in, he said, "Thanks Moira! I appreciate it...I have always wanted to see them. Can't wait to see how you include the washer from *Toys Go Out!*"

I was instantly excited...and glad that he remembered the connection with one of my all-time favorite book series. So after a long day of judging, we headed up to Playhouse Square. It was not only an exciting concert for me but Kit's first concert entirely. I was excited to be able to bring another friend to her first concert! We were also thrilled that the opening act was the Isley Brothers, known for the iconic song "Shout" that is such a rock staple that we've seen it covered by many of the other artists in the book. They were just as great as we had hoped.

The O'Jays themselves were fantastic. They said immediately how excited they were to be back in their home state of Ohio, an honor the state shares with groups like Devo and the Pretenders as well. One of the best rooms in the entire Rock and Roll Hall of Fame pays tribute to some of these artists, and more niche ones as well; it's a really cool thing to check out and even I always learn something about my state's musical history. (Devo is also a favorite of ours—I have a fantastic wooden energy dome in my room that my dad made in wood shop while at West Junior High School in Warren.)

The O'Jays even shared some memories from times they had previously performed in Cleveland. Their entire set was phenomenal. One of my favorite parts was when they paid tribute to Aretha Franklin. Walter Williams, one of the lead singers, had been very close to her and told the audience how frequently they spoke on the phone, right up until the week she passed away. We have great memories of seeing Aretha in concert, so this was really touching, plus it's always cool to hear that your favorite rock stars do know each other and have lives outside of performing onstage!

Besides the music, the O'Jays are of course famous for their dance moves, like many Motown groups. Jordan and Kit had never seen this kind of thing before and thought it was both entertaining and hilarious. Jordan proceeded to walk around our dorm for weeks trying to imitate their moves, much to my amusement.

And of course, the final song of the night was the one I had been waiting for. I love all their songs, but "Love Train" has such a special place in my heart. As the notes began to echo through Playhouse Square, I felt like I was opening up *Toys Go Out*. As we all got into the groove of the song, I felt like I could practically see Lumphy dancing along with the bubbles as Frank the Washing Machine accompanied the band onstage.

—Moira

OUTTAKES

Hall and Oates
May 2014 at Public Hall in Cleveland, Ohio

Hall and Oates' Rock Hall induction in April 2014 stands out vividly in my mind. Questlove of the Roots stepped up to the microphone and declared: "I'm now going to list all of the duets in rock and roll history who have had more of an impact than Hall and Oates. There, I'm done now." Hall and Oates really are the standard.

Being that it was just the two of them making this iconic music it made for some fun when they were being honored as new inductees to the Rock and Roll Hall of Fame. While we did not attend that year, as it was not in Cleveland, we did take the opportunity to go see the simulcast at the Rock Hall. This was the same year the E Street Band was inducted. While they rocked of course due to the number of E Street members honored that night it took over two hours for their induction. When Hall and Oates followed them on stage to give their induction speech one of them stated something like "You are lucky, there are only two of us."

The month after their induction, we would get to see Hall and Oates at Cleveland Public Hall, the same venue used for the inductions when they are held in Cleveland. We had a great view in the 10,000-seat public hall. The venue's main allure is the history that has been on stage. A partial list of the mega acts that have played Cleveland Public Hall includes The Beatles, Elvis Presley, The Doors, The Who, Queen, Led Zeppelin, Cat Stevens, Jerry Lee Lewis, Johnny Cash, Buddy Holly, Chuck Berry, The Jackson Five, and of course on this night, Hall and Oates. Now if you were not convinced already you know why Cleveland Rocks!

Terry's Take

As Hall and Oates sang "Private Eyes," Kim, Moira and the rest of the crowd provided support to the duo with clapping reminiscent of what was done during Cher's "Dark Lady."

That night Hall and Oates rocked "Rich Girl" (my favorite Hall and Oates song) and "Private Eyes" (Kim and Moira's). We felt like we were part of "Live from Daryl's House" the way he and John brought the audience right into their performance. We will forever understand what Questlove meant.   -*Terry*

ELVIS PRESLEY

Elvis Presley Birthday Tribute at Playhouse Square in Cleveland, Ohio:
January 9, 2011; January 9, 2012; January 13, 2013;
January 7, 2014; January 11, 2015; January 10, 2016;
January 8, 2017' January 7, 2018; January 13, 2019

August 15-17, 2013 at the St. George Theatre in Memphis, Tennessee
(International Elvis Tribute Competition)

Moira with Cody Slaughter (left)
and Shawn Klush at Elvis tribute show

"There are two types of people in the world," the tour guide informed us as we walked into Sun Studios on a hot August afternoon. "Elvis fans...and people who haven't heard enough Elvis music."

I was thirteen years old, and we were in Memphis, Tennessee for Elvis Week—a weeklong celebration of all things Elvis. It was the summer before eighth grade and knowing that every summer afterward would be occupied with high school marching band, this was the last chance I would have to make it to Graceland for this particular week in August. And because I had been dreaming of this for years, we booked a trip.

My love of Elvis is all thanks to Jill, my dance teacher since I was six years old. I took dance for thirteen years, which typically surprises anyone I tell because that particular hobby seems at odds with the rest of my personality. But I really loved doing it, and I really really loved our recitals, which always had a creative theme. One year it was one-hit wonders, and for our tap routine, we all jammed to "Jenny Jenny" in

We took a journey all the way to Memphis. Moira at Sun Studios

jean jackets which—when we lined up with our backs to the audience—spelled out "867-5309." Another year, I was Mrs. Potts in the opening number to a Disney-themed show. And when I was ten, the theme was "A Tale of Two Kings": Michael Jackson, the King of Pop, and Elvis Presley, the King of Rock and Roll. My class had two Elvis songs for our routines—"A Little Less Conversation" for jazz and "Jailhouse Rock" for tap. They were the best routines I'd ever learned. I was having so much fun with them that I decided I wanted to practice at home. We went online and bought a CD. It was *Elvis 30 #1 Hits*, with a shiny gold cover, and I immediately began the process of wearing it out completely.

Of course I had heard of Elvis before. It's hard to be a music fan and, quite frankly, an American, without coming across "Blue Suede Shoes" or the image of the black pompadour and gem-studded jumpsuits. But before we ordered that CD, I'd never really listened to his music. There was an entire world beyond that image. From the early "Heartbreak Hotel" and "Don't Be Cruel" through "Way Down" and "The Wonder of You," it spanned his entire career and got me hooked. Soon I had amassed an even bigger collection of his music, diving into the earliest records from Sun Studios and the live recordings from his final concerts in Las Vegas and yes, even the soundtracks to his (objectively terrible) movies.

Obviously, Elvis passed away in 1977, before I was born. However, there's a huge, thriving culture of Elvis tribute artists that I was able to take full advantage of. This has been a source of confusion for many of my friends, who weren't informed. The morning after my first Elvis tribute artist concert, I walked into Prep Bowl practice, exhausted. It had been a pretty late night for an eleven-year-old who wasn't quite used to concerts yet, and it must've showed on my face. My teammate Michael took one look at me and exclaimed, "What happened to you?"

"Elvis concert," I answered tiredly, sliding into a desk.

"You know he's dead, right?" Michael asked, now seeming concerned more for my sanity than my sleep schedule.

Though Michael's *technically* right, Elvis definitely lives through the spirit of these tribute artists. One group of impersonators even fittingly calls themselves the Elvis Lives Tour. There are dozens of ways to see these performers live, from local artists to professionals, but there's a special place in my heart for one in particular: the Elvis Presley Birthday Tribute. We attended the tribute, held at Cleveland's Playhouse Square, each January from 2011 until college put an end to this streak in 2020.

The night always began with Donny Edwards, who would cover all the songs from the 1950s. Then Cody Slaughter would come out in a full black leather jumpsuit to replicate the 1968 Comeback Special. After a brief intermission, Shawn Klush—one of the first ever winners of the International Elvis Tribute Artist Competition—rounds out the night with the iconic Vegas years. There have been some changes

Kim's Commentary

The Elvis Birthday Tribute is top-notch and honors Elvis the best way possible. I must say though it was a bit unsettling when so many females in the crowd, of all ages, were rushing Cody Slaughter as he was performing young Elvis (complete with showering him with kisses and the occasional garment of clothing).

over time—some years we'll get a taste of the eras that Elvis went to Hollywood, occasionally the performers will mix up who does what era, and there are sometimes new additions, like Ryan Pelton, who now handles the Comeback. But it's consistently a great night.

All the performers are also backed by an incredible band led by Juilliard graduate and guitarist Dan Lentino, who serves as emcee, leads the band, and can play the guitar backwards behind his head—a trick that never fails to get the crowd excited. There's also Big Mike, a guitarist and opera singer, and the Sweet Inspirations, two of Elvis's original backup singers. Portia Griffin and Estelle Brown haven't been around lately, as they're getting older, but their vocals are incredible, as are the Blackwood Brothers, a gospel quartet who worked with Elvis. Until his death in 2018, DJ Fontana was also always in attendance. He was Elvis's first drummer, playing for him alongside Bill Black and Scotty Moore, and he would always tell the best stories from touring with the King.

The show only stops in a few cities every year, and we're very lucky that Cleveland is one of them. It's always a special night. After the show, the audience can stick around and meet the performers—so I've gotten to meet all these amazing people as well. I've realized I went to the Stamps-Baxter School of Music with one of the members of the Blackwoods, gotten DJ's autograph on a pair of drumsticks, and now, after nine years, some of them are starting to remember me as a "regular." For example, Ryan Pelton and I have a running joke that he always asks to touch my hair.

My love of Elvis also ended up tying into my love of musical theatre. One of the first shows I ever loved was called *Million Dollar Quartet*, the story of the night of December 4, 1956 when Elvis Presley, Jerry Lee Lewis, Carl Perkins, and Johnny Cash gathered at Sun Studios in Memphis, Tennessee, and had an impromptu jam session. Sam Phillips, the studio owner, had the foresight to turn on one of the recording devices and the night was recorded for posterity. There was a Broadway musical based on it that debuted in 2006 and soon went on tour. I saw it several times throughout its national tour, even building a magazine project in my eighth-grade language arts class around the show. I was actually able to interview several of the cast members for it—a precursor to *Curtain Call*, a magazine by Broadway fans, for Broadway fans that I run today—and visited them backstage when the show came through Toronto.

Martin Kaye as Jerry Lee Lewis, Derek Keeling as Johnny Cash, and Lee Ferris as Carl Perkins were an incredible group, and they were all extremely nice, too. I also got to keep up with Martin Kaye over time as he released music on his own that I started really enjoying. Also, though he wasn't on the tour at the time, but Cody Slaughter had played Elvis on the tour for a time, and I'd gotten to meet him after a different performance. I didn't get to meet the current Elvis, but it was okay—the rest of the cast told me that I could be the fourth member of the quartet.

And then, at the 2019 Birthday Tribute, a new member of the tour brought a real blast from the past.

Back at Elvis Week in 2013, one of the celebration's landmark events was the International Elvis Tribute Artist Competition. After a few years of going to the Birthday Tribute, I had high standards for my Elvis impersonators, and I had studied the competition religiously and knew them all by name by the time we arrived at the first event, a meet and greet at the Memphis Hard Rock Café. I wasn't sure who I would be rooting for, though, until we arrived in the lobby on the first night of competition. Friends and family of the competitors were handing out pennants and buttons in the lobby, and I picked one up for Dean Z—he was who I would cheer on, I decided. And wouldn't you know it, two days later, he was crowned the ultimate champion. Then, my freshman year of college, he had joined the Birthday Tribute tour! At the meet and greet

Moira with Dean Z at Elvis tribute show

afterwards, I told him the story, and he seemed to get a huge kick out of it. And he was still just as great as he was years ago.

That, of course, wasn't the only great memory from Elvis Week. The week was full of great moments. There were panels of those who had worked with him and known him, concerts featuring musicians and singers who performed with him, and screenings of his movies and live concerts. There were also appearances from the DJs on Sirius XM's Elvis Radio, including George Klein, who I had been a fan of for years. He was a pioneer, the Dick Clark of Memphis, who provided racial equality to the performers on his show even in the deeply divided South. He went to high school with Elvis and later became part of his close group of friends known as the Memphis Mafia. He also authored one of the first memoirs I ever fell in love with, which led to memoir being one of my absolute favorite genres to this day.

On the morning of the candlelight vigil, Klein's show was being broadcast from the radio booth at Graceland. I love his show to this day, and I had my copy of his book with me in the hopes that I'd run into him. And sure enough, as we were walking past the booth towards the mansion, we saw him emerge from his book. We joined the small crowd that was gathering around him and I was able to get his autograph and a photo. It was an incredible moment.

But the highlight of the weekend was the candlelight vigil. It's been going on since the year after his death with just a few fans, but now thousands of all ages and backgrounds and homes descend upon Elvis Presley Boulevard. As the sun sets over the gates, golden and reddish light casting a glow over the music notes, the crowd winds up the driveway, past the mansion into the Meditation Garden with candles in hand.

I remember the moment incredibly vividly. The night air was muggy and thick as we trekked to the top of the hill and I took a moment to turn around and look at the crowd behind me. The procession looked like a galaxy, a trail of glittering candles that mirrored the night sky, and I felt myself getting choked up as we passed through the garden and past the graves, which were covered in flowers and memorial displays.

Elvis lives, indeed.

—Moira

QUEEN

July 31, 2019 at the PPG Paints Arena in Pittsburgh, Pennsylvania

Moira with rainbow before Queen concert in Pittsburgh

When we pulled into the parking lot across from PPG Paints Arena, the skies finally cleared. It had been raining for almost the entire drive to Pittsburgh, adding to our string of bad luck with storms over the past month and encouraging my dad's hatred of traveling to Pittsburgh. (Most of his bitterness was about the football team and the number of bridges, which personally I also thought was overkill.) But now it looked like we wouldn't even need umbrellas.

As I got out of the car, I looked up at the arena and noticed a huge rainbow. Not just a few colors smudged across the sky, either, this was a fully formed Roy G. Biv arching over the building.

As my dad joined me, I pointed. "I think that's the spirit of Freddie Mercury."

He smiled. "I think you're right."

A rainbow above a rock concert. The irony wasn't lost on me. Diversity in rock is getting better and better, or at the very least more and more recognized. Just a few years after Cyndi Lauper complained of the issue, more women are being inducted into the Hall of Fame, from Nina Simone to Sister Rosetta Tharpe. Thank you, induction committee, keep it up! But the genre is also over-flowing with heterosexuality.

Growing up, listening to Bryan Adams, Billy Joel, and the Beatles, I noticed that every love song was about a man and a woman. I knew that wasn't about me even before I understood what that meant, but I never saw anything else represented.

It improved as I got older and dug into the history and culture of gay people myself. I found heroes in Harvey Milk, Marsha P. Johnson, and Barbara Gittings, and in the few people in rock who weren't just singing about the opposite sex. There were years when my entire playlist consisted of Little Richard, Elton John, David Bowie, and of course, Freddie Mercury. Once I learned about those artists as people—gay people—their songs resonated with me more than anyone else's. Queen especially. "Somebody to Love," "I Want to Break Free," even the soaring "someone still loves you" in "Radio Ga Ga" felt like the songwriters had jumped into my mind, taken notes, and then splashed the emotions all over the radio. And Freddie Mercury was one of the forces behind it.

I was never lucky enough to see Freddie himself perform. I'm a fan of bands that were popular in the 1950s, 60s, 70s, and 80s and often that means that my favorite artists have passed away or stopped touring. David Bowie, Prince, Johnny Cash, Janis Joplin, Elvis Presley, and Jimi Hendrix are just a few of the artists that I discovered after their deaths and have only experienced through their recordings. If I had a time machine, their concerts are the first places I would go.

Freddie Mercury topped that list. As a frequent visitor to the Rock Hall, I'm always looking forward to the new exhibits on the top two floors, and one of them was *Louder Than Words: Rock, Power, and Politics*. It was about the interconnections between music and history, and part of the exhibit was a video combining clips from

Live Aid and other benefit concerts. I loved the whole thing, but Queen's performance was one of my favorite parts. My dad often told me how much he wished he could've been there for that, and I wished I could've, too.

That may have been the reason it took us so long to see Queen live. We weren't sure anyone could do Freddie justice. It didn't help that we didn't know anything about Adam Lambert. But we eventually decided to buy tickets, partially because we were working on this book and could only think of a few other bands that start with Q such as Quiet Riot. Despite a couple of hits Dad enjoyed, we were not sure if they were even still around. But we are talking Queen here! We shouldn't have worried at all; Adam Lambert was awesome!

From his first words to the audience that night, I fell in love. He just seemed so thrilled to be there. "I'm just like you," he told us, sounding excited. "I'm a fan. This is my dream come true! I can't believe I get to do this every night."

I later learned that he'd auditioned for *American Idol* with "Bohemian Rhapsody" and had mentioned in interviews that he had a poster of Freddie Mercury on his wall as a kid. And when he plainly told us, in a brilliant bit of wordplay, "I get to play with Queen! And I'm a queen," my heart felt like it was going to burst. Here was a performer who wasn't afraid to be himself—to perform "Killer Queen" from the top of a grand piano while flourishing a bright red fan. I instantly knew that he was the perfect person for the role. I took a short video, since my dad and I had both just discovered that it was our shared favorite Queen song and watched it about a thousand times over the next few days.

As the concert continued, I realized he sounded exactly like Freddie including the wildly impressive vocal range. He even had great chemistry with the original members of the band, who were just as impressive to see performing live.

Despite his age, Roger Taylor had more energy than I do and just seemed so thrilled to be up there on stage getting to do this for a living. Brian May was the same way. I have a lot of respect and admiration for Dr. May, who's managed to be both a rock star and an astrophysicist with a thesis topic I don't remotely understand.

And as someone with two majors, three minors, and a habit for both rock concerts and live musical theatre, I relate a lot. Plus, the subtle tribute to his other vocation was amazing: he played a guitar solo on a raised platform, surrounded by lanterns that evoked the planets and accompanied by projections of space and asteroids.

I wasn't the only one who was impressed. An audience can make or break a concert, and luckily, this was one of the best I'd ever experienced. They knew every word, clapped along to "We Will Rock You," and I'd never seen a crowd give so much applause to a guitarist and a drummer. The audience clearly understood that these were gods of rock and roll in front of them.

I'd also never seen so many young people at a concert before. We used to joke that when we turned up for a concert like Frankie Valli and the Four Seasons, I would bring down the median age by a pretty significant margin. It was a huge change, but a welcome one. Some of that was likely due to the huge popularity of the movie *Bohemian Rhapsody*. I remember when it came out; I was studying abroad in Italy at the time and I think I looked up the listings at the Florence American Cinema but didn't want to risk it being in Italian—my translation skills aren't that good—and honestly, I didn't want to see it without my dad.

We went to the movies one of my first days back in the States, which felt quintessentially American: sitting down in a darkened movie theatre with a giant soda (although German Coke is better) and a bucket of popcorn. I really enjoyed the film and got choked up a few times, although I'm a little biased to gay rock stories since they're so relatable and tug pretty hard on my heartstrings (I eagerly went to *Rocketman* a few months later and shed a few tears there, too).

Of course, the popularity also had to do with the song "Bohemian Rhapsody" as well. I don't remember the first time I heard the song. It just feels like it was always ubiquitous, and it was the same way for everyone I knew. I vividly remember the night a group of friends and I, in the car on the way home from Cleveland, immediately burst into song at the top of our lungs when it came on the radio—even though we didn't have any other favorite music in common. And none of us had ever consciously memorized the lyrics. It was like they just appeared in our minds one day, fully formed as if they were handed to us by the ghost of Freddie Mercury himself.

That really extends to all their songs. Our marching band played "Crazy Little Thing Called Love" in high school. When I was in fifth grade, my school's Prep Bowl won the county tournament, and my teammate turned to me and started singing "We Are the Champions." Deeper in their catalog, I realized I also liked their more obscure songs. "39" quickly became one of my favorites. When Brian May walked out onto the stage extension into the crowd and played it on an acoustic guitar, I got chills.

And then, toward the end of the night, when they broke out "Bohemian Rhapsody," it was incredible. There are certain songs that are so brilliant and so ingrained in our culture that seeing them live, after so many renditions on the radio and at public events, it felt like I was somehow hearing it for the first time but with the lyrics screamed in unison by thousands of people.

One of the things I love most about concerts is that each of those thousands of people has a different reason that Queen means something to them. To me, their songs helped me through coming to terms with my sexuality and showed me that I wasn't alone. Before the concert, I talked to the woman next to me, who told me that she had spent over a year hiking through Spain and listened to Queen throughout the whole trip. Down in the pit, there could've been parents and kids who found their first mutual musical connection in Queen, or people who grew up listening to the band and had always dreamed of seeing them live, or even people who had seen the original band when they were younger and finally had the opportunity. I don't know all their stories, but I do know how we sounded singing "Who Wants to Live Forever" with one voice.

—Moira

THE ROLLING STONES

June 20, 2015 at Heinz Field in Pittsburgh, Pennsylvania

Moira gets ready to rock at the Rolling Stones concert in Pittsburgh.
(Note the raincoats...we did not care about the rain
nor did Mick or the rest of the band)

Picking just one band for each letter can be very hard but Moira and I agree: when you are part of the Holy Trinity of British Rock, Wild Horses could not keep the Rolling Stones from this list! We could not believe our luck when we were making summer concert plans that the Rolling Stones were coming so close to home.

Heinz Field in Pittsburgh would be the venue, making this our first ever stadium concert...and what better way to see the Rolling Stones than with 70,000 of your closest friends! Though home to the Pittsburgh Steelers, our beloved Cleveland Browns' longest (and most hated) rival, we could not help but appreciate the customized jerseys available for the Rolling Stones concert that featured the black and gold of the Pittsburgh pro sports teams. What a great concept.

The Rolling Stones are part of one of the more fun questions we like to ask friends and family—as well as complete strangers when appropriate. Beatles or Stones? There's no wiggle room. Nope, you can't respond that your favorite is Bon Jovi or Justin Bieber (please, please don't). You have to pick one or the other. This started for us when I was a teacher and attended the Rock and Roll Hall of Fame Summer Institute for Teachers (which was awesome by the way). The very first question they asked was "Beatles or Stones?" It is a great question if you think about it.

Moira and I have come up with the same nuanced answer... though we can still select one if pressed. We both find that the songs we like by the Rolling Stones really really *love,* but we like more songs by volume by the Beatles. If that makes sense then keep reading; if not please stick with us...this is just how we are.

Some of those Rolling Stones songs that we love include "She's a Rainbow," "Jumpin Jack Flash," "Paint it Black," "Start Me Up," and "Satisfaction." One that I like more than most is "Waiting on a Friend." I can still see my early teen self, watching this video on MTV as it transported me to a block in New York City. At that time, MTV had the power to show us a world in music that we did not know. It was like the internet and social media of its time. We were watching the same thing in Warren, Ohio as they were watching in New York City or Madison, Wisconsin and the entire world seemed accessible to us. Moira's generation will always have the internet for that. We had MTV.

The Rolling Stones toured when I was young, of course, but finances and geography would not make this accessible to me and my friends. The Rolling Stones must have sensed this when, in 1982, they released their "Still Life" concert tour as a film at movie theaters throughout the country. I went and loved it. At that point I had never even been to a concert. I loved the movie and like any eleven-year-old I pretended like I was there. I am certain I was singing with them and maybe even a little air guitar. I do not remember who I went with...I wish I did. It was an awesome show even though on the big screen and not live.

Back in Pittsburgh in the present, a newer band called AwolNation opened for the Stones. They were great. I remarked to Moira how the lead singer kept reminding the massive audience of their name between songs and how that was smart in a corporate sense. She gave me the same look she gave me when I remarked to her at the ocean one time. Upon seeing a cargo ship, I said, "I am glad God made the seas for commerce." I think her look indicated each time that my comment was way too corporate of a remark for the natural wonder before us—whether the breadth of the ocean or a Rolling Stones concert.

AwolNation finished their set and ushered in the iconic Rolling Stones! They opened with "Jumpin Jack Flash" and rocked many more of our favorites: "Brown Sugar," "Paint it Black," "Start Me Up," and "Satisfaction." One of the highlights of the evening was when the Penn State choir took the stage to back them up on "You Can't Always Get What You Want." As Moira would write in our journal—which we affectionately still refer to as the "baby book"—the Penn State choir backing up the Stones was "Beautiful and absolutely amazing."

Our seats were the second section back from the stage but in the first row of that section...they afforded a great view of the full band. We could clearly see the legendary Rolling Stones and we could hear them so well that the threshold shift that my speech language pathologist wife warned me about would end up kicking in for a few days.

We even had some rain come in for our first stadium concert, but it did not dampen the mood or lessen the antics and music of Mick and the boys. Moira and I refer to the video of American Bandstand that plays at the Rock and Roll Hall of Fame a lot and often recite the words of Little Richard on that video when Dick Clark asks him "Who are the new up and coming band in England?" with Little Richard answering "The Rolling Stones." Over fifty years later and this has not changed...the Rolling Stones was an experience well worth the wait.

—*Terry*

OUTTAKES

REO Speedwagon
June 2013 at the Ohio State Fair in Columbus, Ohio

A child of the '70s and '80s vinyl albums will always bring back great musical memories and REO Speedwagon's *Hi-Infidelity* is right up there with one of the best from beginning to end. I will share the other half of the night with you in the very next section (spoiler alert: it's Styx), but REO Speedwagon was as awesome live as that album was on my turntable in one of our rental houses in Warren! Kevin Cronin showed he does not age and led the group with what I can only think was the same energy as he did in the '80s. He would later add new memories for me: during the COVID-19 Pandemic he started a weekly online program called "Camp Cronin." Detailing his and the band's experiences, and providing a preview to a book he was working on, it helped me get through the dark days of 2020. REO Speedwagon was another band on my list for a long time and Moira and I agreed we are going to keep on loving REO Speedwagon.   *-Terry*

Lionel Richie
August 2016 at the Covelli Centre in Youngstown, Ohio

Not surprisingly many non-concert goers and occasional ones were out in full force to see Lionel Richie in Youngstown. His ballads are forever imprinted on my generation. I loved his Commodore hits and Kim was more in tune with the later ballads but we both loved the show as did Moira. "Say You Say Me," "Endless Love," "Hello," "Stuck on You," "Dancing on the Ceiling," "Penny Love," and more were all shared with us from this music legend as we rocked "All Night Long."   *-Terry*

Kenny Rogers
December 2013 at Packard Music Hall in Warren, Ohio

In high school, I was on the speech and debate team—which has far fewer connections to rock and roll than other activities I did, like marching band. But during my senior year, I mentored a younger team member in my category by the name of Calvin. I adored Calvin, but I think I made him nervous. It took weeks into the season before he let me watch him perform. When I did, I was blown away. His intro, and the overarching theme of his speech, was Kenny Rogers' "The Gambler." It was delivered perfectly and every time he spoke the lyrics, I was sent back to the time we saw Kenny Rogers live in concert, in the winter of 2013, when he performed not only his hits but several Christmas songs. Now I have two great memories attached to the song.   *-Moira*

Runaway Saints
July 2015 at Huntington Convention Center in Toledo, Ohio

Opening acts are tricky. Sometimes, there's a double bill where it seems like nobody is really an opening act—I mean, can you really say whether Joan Jett or the Who are the bigger, better band? Sometimes, though, the opener is unremarkable and within a few weeks you can't even remember who played before the main performer took the stage. Sometimes there's a welcome surprise. That was the case with the Runaway Saints. This folksy rock band opened for Rod Stewart and during the break before he took the stage, we found ourselves humming their songs. We bought a CD and met the band, who were very sweet. We still occasionally listen to that CD and they have remained, without a doubt, our favorite opening act. Rod Stewart himself was also fantastic. He apologized after the first song, telling us that he had been under the weather, but we couldn't even tell as he charged through his greatest hits and even kicked autographed soccer balls into the crowd!   *-Terry*

STYX

July 28, 2013 at the Ohio State Fair in Columbus, Ohio

June 27, 2018 at Blue Hills Bank Pavilion in Boston, Massachusetts

Styx was another one of my early favorite bands as I became a fan of Rock and Roll. Of course, they like several others Moira and I have seen on this A to Z journey—they had a song on the Rock Album my Uncle Ted gave me back when I was nine or ten. Moira too became a fan of Styx early on, due in large part to having shared their songs on car rides to the park, to our beloved Borders Bookstore, to dance class, and pretty much everywhere.

It is hard not to get excited when you hear "Renegade," "Come Sail Away," "Rockin the Paradise," and pretty much their entire songbook. This Styx concert at the Ohio State Fairgrounds was one of our early concert-going experiences together. Or, as Moira puts it, "One of the first times I felt that energy." Stepping up right after REO Speedwagon, who also blew the crowd away (see R Outtake, page 122), Styx hit the stage what had to be the same energy as their early concerts.

Sometimes rock concerts are about the crowds nearly as much as the artists. We have been at shows where the crowds were on the lamer side. The crowd on this night at the Celeste Center at the Ohio State Fairgrounds were in tune with the band and rocked all night with them.

While Dennis Deyoung had not been with the band for a while, we did get to see original members Chuck Panozzo, James "J.Y." Young, and legendary guitarist Tommy Shaw who joined the band in 1975. The presence of them and the backing of several other awesome performers, including lead singer Lawrence Gowan who joined the band in 1999, this is still a concert we talk about often.

One of the nice surprises we had that night was Gowan's intermission montage of classic rock favorites. He brings an energy that few in the business do and the crowd responded in kind. I would later take Kim to see Styx at a Youngstown stop on their tour and the rock montage was as good as ever.

We walked away from that first Styx concert in Columbus with a nice surprise too. At the end of the concert the drummer launched his drumsticks in the air and they landed near us. I went for it immediately and when coming up with it another guy tried to take it out of my hand. I stood my ground and the other guy stood down and we walked away with sticks from Styx. Those drum sticks now have a place of honor with autographed ones from Elvis Presley's drummer D.J. Fontana.

Styx also invokes memories of one of our favorite television shows that lasted just one season. The show *Freaks and Geeks* chronicled the lives of high school teens in the '80s. An early Judd Apatow work that is very underrated and left us way too early. Though other '80s music was used in the show, Styx was a favorite and played during some of the show's most memorable scenes. Fans of the show will recall the character Nick singing "Lady" to Lindsey (Freaks) to express his teenage love to her. "Renegade" was well placed too, as characters Neil and Bill (Geeks) prepared themselves for a "fight." To me the most memorable scene of the series, as well as the most moving, was set to "Come Sail Away," as the character Lindsey dances with Eli, a special needs student who suffers from being singled out negatively during the show. To me this remains one of the most moving scenes that I have seen on television.

Moira and I would see Styx again with Joan Jett and Tesla in Boston and they would deliver yet again an awesome concert. If you ever get a chance to see Styx while they are still touring you will be in for "The Best of Times."

—*Terry*

OUTTAKES

Bob Seeger
December 2014 at Quicken Loans Arena in Cleveland, Ohio

Bob Seeger and the Silver Bullet Band is another that had been on my list for a long time. "Old Time Rock and Roll" is a favorite of all classic rockers. When you see him live, you find yourself saying "Wow...I forgot he sang that too" over and over again. "Against the Wind" is one of my favorite songs of all time, while "Mainstreet"—with some of the best sax solos of all time—still rings in my ears from that night.

Being there with Kim and Moira to see Bob Seeger and the Silver Bullet Band was a perfect night for our family. And it didn't hurt that J. Geils Band was the opening act!   *-Terry*

Southside Johnny and the Asbury Jukes
August 2013 at the Warren Community Amphitheater in Warren, Ohio
November 2019 at the Hard Rock Café in New York, New York

Another great venue that has been built as part of a renaissance in the downtown of our hometown (Warren, Ohio). I was introduced to Southside Johnny of course by Bruce Springsteen as most hardcore fans of the boss and the E Street Band were. Closely associated with the New Jersey music scene, Southside Johnny is known for horn-driven bluesy Rock and—as we found that night—he's quite awesome on the harmonica too. The Warren Amphitheater typically hosts some of the best tribute bands in the country, but this night we got to see the actual Southside Johnny and the Asbury Jukes. We hope he liked Warren as much as Warren enjoyed them. We got to see Southside Johnny again later with Stevie Van Zandt as part of a fundraising gala for Stevie's Rock and Roll Forever Foundation. Southside Johnny rocks!   *-Terry*

Terry's Take

Sunrise Pizza is a staple in Warren, Ohio so it did not surprise us when they were involved building a concert series around the downtown development of the amphitheater. It is great to see city leaders step up and make quality of life a priority.

126

Michael Stanley and the Resonators
October 2013 at Packard Music Hall in Warren, Ohio

Michael Stanley is the Cleveland counterpart to Pittsburgh's Donnie Iris and the Cruisers. This connection is made often, and the bands have had many nights together sharing a stage over four decades. The Mahoning Valley where we live is in the middle of Cleveland and Pittsburgh. This result in not only being exposed to great bands from each mid-sized city but also made for some interesting back and forth between Browns and Steelers fans.

Growing up in the late '70s/early '80s, the success of the Steelers and the struggles of our Cleveland Browns made it tough on us loyal Browns fans. We had to deal with some good-natured ribbing quite often due to our geography. Once the late '80s came around the Browns would have their day. Us diehard Browns fans will not soon forget the dual 1,000 yard rushers of Kevin Mack and Ernest Byner and the accuracy of the arm of Mahoning Valley native Bernie Kosar. We're still waiting on that Super Bowl though.

Michael Stanley is the quintessential Cleveland rock band. Growing up, it was the Michael Stanley Band, or MSB, which later gave way to Michael Stanley and the Resonators. His songs instantly bring back memories of listening to one of the best and biggest rock radio stations in the nation: 100.7 FM WMMS (The Buzzard!). His songs "My Town," "He Can't Love You," and "Lover" had some minor success nationally but are staples of classic rock in Cleveland. The song "Lover" still has one of my favorite lines ever in a song and one that speaks to all of us in Northeast Ohio "Thank God for the man who put the white lines on the highway." There is a story, that I have heard but not confirmed, that he came up with that driving back to Cleveland from Youngstown in the Mahoning Valley.

For quite a while, his steady gig has been as a Dee Jay on Cleveland's 98.5 FM. I would have loved to have had taken Moira and Kim to see him in Cleveland. Not too long after I would see the Cleveland legend again with a friend of mine, Mark, who has great taste in music and a knowledge base about it (and other things) that at times is truly astounding. That night we would see Michael Stanley with Donnie Iris at the Hard Rocksino Northfield Park (now the MGM Northfield Casino), a sore subject with Moira as it was a venue she won't be able to get into until she is 21.

Going to concerts with Kim and Moira, as you can tell, has been one of the true joys in my life. Having great friends is another. Sharing concerts with friends—as well as sporting events and fun times in our living room playing board games—Kim, Moira, and I have been blessed to have made our journey through Rock and Roll (and life) even richer.   *-Terry*

Ringo Starr and His All Starr Band
October 2015 at Heinz Hall in Pittsburgh, Pennsylvania
June 2016 at Riverbend Music Center in Cincinnati, Ohio

We cannot believe our luck that we have been able to see the two living Beatles. We were able to see Ringo get inducted into the Rock and Roll Hall of Fame, which of course is impossible to beat, but seeing him with his All Starr Band is a great experience. Not only did he play his solo hits but he has put together a great band who played some of their hits as well.

The set list and band were equally good at both shows, featuring Ringo classics like "Photograph" and "It Don't Come Easy." But part of the fun is that the All Starr band features musicians from other legendary acts, many of whom led them through their own hits. With Steve Lukather of Toto, the band powered through "Rosanna," "Africa" and "Hold the Line." Behind Gregg Rolie of Santana, they played "Evil Ways." Todd Rungren rocked through "Bang on the Drum all Day" and teased his mega-hit "Hello it's Me." Mr. Mister's Richard Page led "Kyrie" and "Broken Wings." On top of that they played several Beatles classics, including "Yellow Submarine" and "With a Little Help from My Friends."

The Cincinnati show was even more exciting as we got to share this concert with my niece Morgan. Morgan and Moira have always been close. One of the things that they bonded over most have been their taste in music. Morgan loves the Beatles, always has, and it was awesome to have her join us. Plus, she and Moira ended up at the front near the end of the show. Peace and Love to Ringo as he rocked PA and Ohio that night!   *-Terry*

Moira with cousin Morgan

Steely Dan
July 2015 at Blossom Music Center in Cuyahoga Falls, Ohio

Steely Dan's music is a soul-filled and mostly mellow sound featuring iconic lyrics. I can't think of Steely Dan without my mind going to a beloved local bookstore we had in our town before it closed. As a family we spent many days at this Borders Bookstore and I recall one time being in line and seeing a Steely Dan anthology set at the register. On the CD collection, I saw the name of one of my friends who we affectionately refer to as Mayor Mike. I waited until after the holidays to confirm it was his...and then I heard how much he loved the band.

We were lucky to see what he was talking about live as we enjoyed "Rikki Don't Lose that Number," "Dirty Work," "Do it Again," and "Reelin in the Years." The crowd loved it as much as I'm sure Mayor Mike would have. *-Terry*

Steve Miller Band
July 2013 at the Ohio State Fair in Columbus, Ohio

Steve Miller Band's Greatest Hits 1974-78 is one of the best albums from front to back ever. This is one standard that I recall having the 8-track version (courtesy of my mom and dad), the album, and (later) the CD. The CD of Steve Miller Band's greatest hits helped get me through starting out living in my first apartment as an adult with no cable. Regardless of what format you listen to, you can easily identify what song is coming next.

I was beginning to think I would never get to see him. But when the State Fair released their concert schedule—something we look forward to annually—we were excited to learn that Steve Miller Band would be there. The band did not disappoint one bit. Moira and I loved it! It was also the 30th anniversary of the iconic album "The Joker," so most of that album was played and it was incredible.

-Terry

Rod Stewart
July 2015 at the Huntington Convention Center in Toledo, Ohio

Rod Stewart was a rocker who was as high up on Kim's list as mine. We all headed West from the Mahoning Valley to Toledo to see him. We did make sure to stop at the iconic Tony Packos, made famous in Toledo by the MASH character Max Klinger (played by Toledo native Jamie Farr) as that was on the non-musical bucket list. We then made our way to the Huntington Convention Center.

Rod Stewart put on a great show, belting out all his hits including "Maggie May" and "You're in my Heart." We also found out that night when he started kicking autographed soccer balls into the crowd, that he was not only a soccer fan but was part owner of a professional team! *-Terry*

Kim's Commentary

When Terry mentions MASH, I cannot help but think of a "pop-up" museum I agreed to go with him to in Dayton to see a private held collection of MASH memorabilia. When he was on his third hour there talking to the owner/operator, we discovered that the longest anyone had been there was about a half hour prior to that visit. I began to worry we would inherit this collection.

Straight No Chaser
November 2011 at Playhouse Square in Cleveland, Ohio

For the uninitiated Straight No Chaser is not your traditional rock band but more of an a cappella group that rocks! They began their careers in the mid-'90s at Indiana University and hit it big when their video of the iconic Christmas song "The Twelve Days of Christmas," sang in their unique way, went viral. We loved the show and the accessibility of the band. We met all of them at their merch table afterwards and they were really sweet.   *-Moira*

George Thorogood / The Tallest Man on Earth

What to do with the letter T? So far, we've done so well narrowing down and agreeing on one band for every letter, but here we are deadlocked on T. Our connections to two musicians were just too strong for either of us to give up, so we could not find a way to break the tie. As you read about our strong love for George Thorogood (Terry) and The Tallest Man on Earth (Moira), we think you'll see why.

George Thorogood
June 2, 2015 at the Rose Music Center in Huber Heights, Ohio

I just need to put it out there that any moment George Thorogood comes on the radio, I must listen. Whether "Bad to the Bone" (an album my dad owned), "Move it on Over," "I Drink Alone," or "One Bourbon, One Scotch, One Beer"—one of my all-time favorites—something about his music hits me with waves of nostalgia.

When we had the chance to head to Huber Heights, just outside of Dayton, Ohio, it was on. We had to go. We knew we would be seeing what seemed like an odd double bill though. I love the Stray Cats and Brian Setzer, but I thought Brian Setzer and George Thorogood...different audiences, for the most part. But we liked both so off we went.

I had been wanting to see George Thorogood ever since the likely hundred times or so I listened to my dad's album with "Bad to the Bone" on it. The music connected to me as it connected to things I would experience in my childhood. Being that the adults in my family were young and alcohol was a staple of their beverage diet, the themes in his music hit home. The song "One Bourbon, One Scotch, One Beer" being at the top of the list.

Right off the bat he is talking about the landlady. And not unlike many of the kids I would go to elementary school with, I remember growing up in the City of Warren living in apartment complexes and rental houses. That seemed to be the norm but what was not the norm among my friends was moving to a different one seemingly every year. This lasted from the time I was born until I was about fourteen and entering my freshman year of high school when we had moved for the 14th time. What I figured out was we were likely a few months behind on our rent. Or, to put it bluntly, we were not paying our rent.

My parents were young and doing the best they could. Moving often resulted in the experience of having a friend over and my dad appearing at my bedroom door a week or less in advance of the move saying, "Get things packed up, we are moving again." One time I remember my friend turning glum and me saying, "Don't worry, it is probably close by and I'll still be at the same elementary school." It was on a street nearby so that time my dad and his friend Ziggy would carry our swingset down the street, not needing a truck as the new rental house was so close. And yes, Rock and Roll fans, my dad's buddy Ziggy was nicknamed after Bowie's Ziggy Stardust.

George Thorogood's quest to convince his landlady and his friend's wife to "stay a couple of days" was not lost on this boy from Warren. We had a few houseguests a day at a time, particularly in my younger days and experienced many of the things those with very young parents do.

Being a classic rock fan and loving this song so much it may surprise you that I am a teetotaler. I do not drink alcohol at all. From an early age, I was weary to begin drinking so as I had example after example in my life of people who were prone to addiction. It was sad to me that people I loved became different people entirely when under the influence of alcohol and drugs. I wanted to make sure I never went down that road. Though alcohol and other things would be accessible, seeing what it did to some of those in my life was a constant reminder that it was not for me. If I started down that road just for fun would I ever be able to stop? There were many experiences that reinforced this but one when I was third grade served as an ultimate reminder for me.

My family hosted several people for a party to watch a championship boxing match at our house. While some went out on the town, others stayed at our house to watch the boxing...mostly split by the men and women. At some point in the night several ran out to the store. When pulling out of the driveway, a drunk driver hit the car. The daughter of one of my parent's friends, who we were just playing with, tragically died right in front of our house. It is an image that I can't easily let go of and is another reason I do not drink to this day.

It took me awhile to warm up to the fact that most people can drink alcohol and not be addicted or make bad decisions. I am blessed with the best group of friends you can have, and they are exactly the kind of people who have shown me that consumption certainly can be controlled as can actions by those drinking. I think back to my early twenties, hanging out at an awesome local bar in Warren called Little Wing Café, embracing a Dr. Pepper while we all jam to George Thorogood. Moira has had similar experiences— when she studied abroad, many of her friends in the program tried Italian wine, German beer, Irish whiskey, and more of the local alcohol. She was a little worried at first that they would pressure her into drinking, but they were great and cheered her on as she tried Coke in ten different countries! One even bought her a wineglass with "Coke Connoisseur" on it. It's a good thing to be comfortable not drinking around drinkers, as Classic Rock concerts are not the place to be if alcohol bothers you.

Despite not being a drinker, I still identify with George Thorogood's music. Like everyone else, I went crazy when he started singing that night. As he began, he quickly said to the crowd, "I think you have heard this song before," before launching into "One Bourbon, One Scotch, One Beer." It was a great night and like any great music took me back to my younger days...both good times and times that I had to work through to move forward.

He may not fit her to a "T," but Moira and I agree that George Thorogood is "Bad to the Bone"!

—*Terry*

The Tallest Man on Earth

September 3, 2015 at the House of Blues in Cleveland, Ohio

May 10, 2019 at the Carnegie of Homestead Music Hall in Pittsburgh, Pennsylvania

The summer before my seventh grade year, I fell head over heels in love with the musical *Newsies*. It told the story of newsboys, in 1899 in New York City, who rebelled against a price hike by newspaper owners with a strike. The show alone inspired me—the rise of the less privileged, fighting for their rights and winning against odds that seemed impossible. I absolutely blame this show, and songs like "The World Will Know," "Watch What Happens," and "Once and for All" for my activism and burning desire to overthrow the system.

The community around *Newsies* also became incredibly important to me. This show introduced me to a group who were different and just didn't care what anyone thought. They were queer, they loved theatre, they had a crazy hodgepodge of interests and identities and they bonded, they lived, anyway. I was beginning my own coming-out process, and coming to terms with how different, and at times outcast, I felt. But these people were different, too, and they'd formed a family out of it. It was a far-flung family that only

Moira with Fansies

united every once in a while, at the Nederlander Theatre, but it felt like home to me.

Newsies also introduced me to the rest of Broadway. When the show closed in August 2013, I followed many of the cast members to their new jobs, and soon, I had been bitten by the Broadway bug and there was no going back.

Throughout that time (and even now when I'm feeling nostalgic), I consumed every bit of *Newsies*-related content that I could, including Andrew Keenan-Bolger's iconic vlogs chronicling the show's journey from Paper Mill Playhouse in New Jersey to Broadway and beyond. Several of these also followed the cast's personal adventures, and one of these was called #FallRoadTrip.

The video has a really warm and fuzzy vibe with scenes from a vacation upstate to a farm. It chronicles good times that many experience, such as spending time with friends on the road. *Newsies* fans rejoiced as we followed their exploits. It had the same familial feel of the fandom and it was set to a great song called "1904," by a musician who went by the stage name "the Tallest Man on Earth." I decided to look more into him.

He had three albums at the time: *Shallow Grave*, *The Wild Hunt*, and *There's No Leaving Now*. They had incredibly poetic lyrics packed with stunning imagery; they were part folk and part indie, bordering on rock at times, and completely different from most of the other music that I listened to. They sound melancholy to a degree, but listening to the lyrics reveals stories upon stories and incredible layers of emotion expressed in beautiful, almost figurative, language.

It was also completely different listening to a contemporary artist. Yes, I'll listen to the newer albums of my favorite older artists—Joan Jett's *Unvarnished* from 2015 is one of my favorites of all time. But to enjoy the music of someone who was constantly releasing new music (and had an actual social media presence that didn't seem to be run by a public relations person who understood social media in a way that the older band members never could) was a new experience for me. This opened the door into other modern bands and musicians who I now count among my favorites, just as much as Springsteen or Styx.

The music of the Tallest Man on Earth immediately became a staple of my playlists, from the classics to the newer "Dark Bird is Home" and "I Love You, It's a Fever Dream." In particular, he was one of the main people I listened to while I wrote. It was a calming backdrop and an inspiring one. My main genre is poetry, and sometimes there's nothing to jumpstart a poem like a beautiful song. I also started teaching myself some favorites on my ukulele.

The hospital where I spent my time with Stevens-Johnson Syndrome had expressions therapy, which is an incredible service. They gave me free coloring pages, had a room devoted to the arts for patients, and even sent a therapist to teach me how to play ukulele. It was one of the only things that helped me stay sane throughout a difficult experience, and I'm grateful to everyone there for getting me through. It's still a way that I express myself, though I mostly stick to old folk protest songs from the sixties.

I've been lucky enough to see the Tallest Man on Earth—whose name is actually Kristian Matsson—twice in concert. We saw him for the first time during my freshman year of high school in a venue that was brand new to me: the Cleveland House of Blues. It's a very cool place, and we'd been walking past it for years because the restaurant entrance is in the Fourth Street Alley, one of our favorite parts of Cleveland.

The area is home to a lot of really cool restaurants and shops, including Cleveland Clothing Company. That's where I've picked up my absolute favorite t-shirts over the years, including the WMMS eagle, a skeleton riding a surfboard with the phrase "Burning River Surf Club," and two shirts to wear when the Browns and Indians are playing (the Browns one says "Let's go football! Hit a home run"; the Indians one says, "Let's go baseball! When is halftime?"). It also leads right up to Quicken Loans Arena, better known as the Q, where the Cavs play (technically, it's now called the Rocket Mortgage Field House, but I absolutely refuse to call it that). We spent a lot of time in the area during the 2016 Republican National Convention, which was held in Cleveland, as I joined my dad when he took his students there to experience some of the activities surrounding the convention—many of the news outlets set up and reported from locations along the alley, including CNN, who turned a restaurant called Harry Buffalo into the CNN Café.

Fourth Street Alley is also a cool place in terms of its history. Founder Isaac Tigrett, who grew up on the blues in Tennessee, wanted to introduce it to the rest of the world. He opened the first House of Blues in 1992, in a historic home in Cambridge, Massachusetts, with not only live music and traditional delta cuisine, but also folk art. This folk, outsider, and self-taught art is called the "visual blues" and they are the largest curator of these forms of art in the world. For example, the curtains on the stage in Cleveland are quilted in the Jacob's Ladder pattern to pay respect to the enslaved African Americans who used the Underground Railroad as a passage to freedom. Under the stage, not just in Cleveland but in every House of Blues, is a metal box full of mud from the Mississippi to "ensure that every artist has the roots and the spirit of the South planted beneath their feet."

They also run a charity called Music Forward, which focuses on underrepresented young people and provides workshops and showcases to inspire them to pursue careers in the music industry. They're extremely committed to community, feeding the homeless on Thanksgiving, supporting local artists, and more.

Additionally, though it's built on concepts taken from juke joints and has the communal vibe of a bar with live music, I'm allowed in the House of Blues even though I'm under 21. I've always been very frustrated by venues like the Hard Rock Café's line of casinos, which bring in incredible acts like Diana Ross, but don't allow anyone underage even into the restaurant and concert venue sections of their buildings. So having a venue like this that I can access is wonderful.

The concert was fantastic. Seeing an indie artist was cool and different. Sometimes, when we see a classic rock act, it feels as though there are certain songs that they have to include—and for good reason, because if I saw Journey and they didn't sing "Don't Stop Believing," I'd be pretty upset. Then they'll drop in some from their new album, some more obscure favorites, and maybe some audience requests. There are certainly artists who break this pattern, like the E Street Band, but the Tallest Man on Earth really seemed to just be playing what he wanted. Personally, I really like that approach to a concert—and when you like all of the songs, none of which ever made it big on the radio, there's nothing to complain about when something doesn't get played unless they leave out their personal favorite.

Which he didn't and that was okay. It was still a great night. We decided to see him again a few years later. It was the last day of my freshman year of college, which had been an absolutely wild ride—I'd spent the first semester studying in Florence, Italy, and then came to the university in Kent, Ohio after the first snow had buried practically all of campus. Spring semester couldn't have been more different, and the adjustment was sometimes hard. Thankfully, I loved all my classes and made connections that resulted in making the next year a million times easier, but by the end, I was ready for summer break. And after packing all my belongings into my grand-parents' van and moving it into the living room, we decided to deal with all of it later and go to a concert. Because that's what we do.

It was the Carnegie Library of Homestead, which was one of many similar libraries Andrew Carnegie built across the country. This one has a pool and a concert hall. We'd never been there before and instantly loved it. It's a huge, old, regal-looking building that's been incredibly well-preserved and is honestly one of my favorite venues of all time. And that night was genuinely one of my all-time favorite concerts.

I've talked before about how sometimes there is just magic in the air at a concert and that concert had it. The crowd was excited, Kristian was full of passion, and the music filling the ancient wood-en rafters charged the hall with a special kind of energy. And when he sat down at the piano for one of the final songs of the night, he cued up my favorite song, "Kids on the Run."

For those few hours, it seemed like the past twelve months—all the happiness, sadness, and overwhelming emotions and change—poured out of the piano, the guitar, and the voices of the performer and the crowd. It was the culmination of everything I love about live music.

—Moira

OUTTAKES

James Taylor
January 2013 at the US Capitol in Washington
(2nd Inauguration of President Obama)

My dad is a former social studies teacher and raised me to believe that democracy is a verb. This is not just a motto; he puts it into practice every day, even as an administrator, taking students to rallies, debates, hosting speakers like free speech hero Mary Beth Tinker and even taking students to the Iowa Caucus and the Inauguration. I got to go with him one year when he was not chaperoning a group of students, though

Moira with Mary Beth Tinker

we were joined by some recent graduating students he previously had in class. We attended President Barack Obama's second Inauguration in 2013. We stood, shivering in the early-morning DC air, for hours until the ceremony started. A welcome surprise in addition to the history in the making was a performance by James Taylor.   *-Moira*

Teaching social studies is the best! The goal was to make it come alive for students...as Moira shared "Democracy is a Verb." So many teachers, elected officials, community activists and willing students were part of this as we invited officials into the schools, attended presidential debates, headed out to Iowa for students to work on campaigns and experience the Iowa Caucus first-hand, and attend presidential inaugurations. We also attended several speeches. Some of the most memorable ones were taking students to see actor

Martin Sheen and Mary Beth Tinker joining us for Democracy Day. Over the years both have been supportive of student efforts to engage with their government. I can't thank them enough for their inspiration!   *-Terry*

Actor Martin Sheen meeting Pat Hogan, Terry's secretary while he was Superintendent at Lordstown

Tesla
June 2018 at the Blue Hills Bank Pavillion in Boston, Massachusetts

You are not a child of the '80s if you don't know Tesla. Though the number of songs most of us could name is limited, "Love Song" will forever be part of high school dance memories. It was exciting hearing it live along with "Signs." I am going out of on a limb here and say I like it better than the original by Five Man Electric Band (I did have to look that up. They were opening up for Styx and Joan Jett and the Blackhearts that night in Boston, but we did get to see Tesla doing these two '80s favorites.   *-Terry*

Three Part Invention
January 2011 at the Akron Public Library in Akron, Ohio

The outtakes of letter B included Jim Brickman, the classical pianist, who was almost forgotten by my mom and I because his violinist Tracy Silverman was just so cool. My dad, though a little incredulous at first, brought us to see Tracy's instrumental group at an art museum just a few months later. To this day, if my dad hears that Jim Brickman is coming nearby, he'll tell me and my mom...and our immediate response is always "Is Tracy Silverman with him?"   *-Moira*

U2

June 7, 2017 at Heinz Field in Pittsburgh, Pennsylvania

2017 was the 30th anniversary of the album *The Joshua Tree* by U2, a band still on our bucket list. We were thrilled to hear that the Bono-led band would be coming to both Cleveland and Pittsburgh as part of their tour performing *Joshua Tree* from beginning to end. Unfortunately, the date in Cleveland did not work. Our hometown in the Mahoning Valley is right in the middle of Cleveland and Pittsburgh so we got the tickets right away to see U2.

Moira was familiar with them as I had a copy of their CD *All That You Can't Leave Behind* and played it a great deal in the car. The CD came out in October 2000. At that time Moira would have been six months old. I had decided to go back to school to get my teaching license and this would also enable me to be more of a "stay at home Dad" while she was little. From a young age, she got to hear what I personally feel is U2's best album and one of my favorite songs that led off the CD *Beautiful Day*. She even said when she was talking a few years later, "Let's listen to *Beautiful Day* music."

The concert would bring us back for a second stadium show at Heinz Field in Pittsburgh, Pennsylvania. In terms of contemporary bands, The Lumineers are one that we like, and we see them as more "old school rock" than most other bands. As U2's opening act, they did not disappoint. They were a great lead in for U2.

I have always said to Moira that Bono is like the European Bruce Springsteen. His songs speak to people like Bruce's do and he is seen like a folk hero in his home country much like Bruce. Bono continues to be an activist and has helped many through his efforts. His advocacy work, with AIDS and poverty and for groups like Amnesty International, make him a folk hero to many and represents what is right with the world of music (when U2 is involved). This is one reason some refer to Bono as the European Bruce Springsteen. Interestingly, it was Bruce who inducted U2 into the Rock and Roll Hall of Fame.

On that night and throughout their tour, the band highlighted famous women. After finishing the eleven-song set that makes up *The Joshua Tree* album they shared images of women who have made an impact on history through trailblazing women of herstory. It was very inspiring for Moira and I both.

Icons from music—such as Grace Jones and Patti Smith—as well from politics and history—such as First Lady Michelle Obama, Secretary of State Condolezza Rice, and trans rights activist Marsha P. Johnson—were all celebrated, along with many others. As we would read later, the photos were part of a project called "Herstory," using feminist art to engage people of all genres with women's history. We also found photos from the tour and one included Cleveland's own rock journalist Jane Scott!

U2 has consistently remained a great rock band. I hope the band can stay together for years to come just as I hope that Bruce Springsteen and the E Street Band do. Both continue to pave the way for bands advocating for their fellow man and women.

—Terry

STEVIE VAN ZANDT

**November 2019 at the Hard Rock Café in New York, New York
(Rock and Roll Forever Foundation Gala)**

*Moira and Terry with one of our all-time favorite rockers
and an advocate for educators Stevie Van Zandt*

With two parents working in the schools from as early as I can remember, I've been very involved in different types of education advocacy. My mom and dad raised me to understand the importance of not only different educational topics, such as inclusion of the arts and funding for schools, but also how vital it is to let your representatives in government know what you think. It didn't matter that I couldn't vote yet, either. I was writing letters through tools like Resistbot far before I turned eighteen, and making my opinions known in other ways. I remember when I was in third grade, I put up a sign in my locker against Senate Bill 5 in Ohio. This bill took rights away from teachers and other public employees.

The arts in the schools have always been one of the most important issues to our family. I was very lucky that my school had excellent arts offerings from elementary through high school and our county provided additional programs like Saturday Enrichment and—my personal favorite—Arts Excel. Participants in this program were excused from school on Fridays for an entire day of instruction on whatever artistic subject we were most interested in, from the visual arts to dance to music to drama.

Unfortunately, many school districts are not so lucky, whether that's because of a lack of value of the arts or a lack of funding for programs like this. I've seen it get worse over time. There's such an emphasis on STEM nowadays, which is undoubtedly important. But forgetting the humanities and the arts is downright dangerous, not just for kids who need it, but also for society as a whole. I've seen my parents in their own jobs try very hard to include the arts in their own lessons and encourage their coworkers to do the same. And that is where Stevie Van Zandt comes in.

He runs the Rock and Roll Forever Foundation and their Teach Rock initiative. Many prominent rockers serve on the Board of Directors, including Jackson Browne, Bruce Springsteen, and Bono. TeachRock provides wonderful teacher support and quality curriculum and materials.

Of course, many of the lesson plans are about the genres that more closely tie into Rock and Roll, such as social studies. It's incredibly easy to connect history and current events with the music of different periods! But there are also STEM-related lessons about the different technologies involved in Rock and Roll, like the physics of sound and instrument evolution. Language arts plans can include a discussion of how the Harlem Renaissance and beat poetry went hand in hand with black musicians and 60s musical counterculture. Analyzing lyrics like Dylan's from a literary perspective. Art curriculum relating color theory to band logos and album covers. The list goes on.

There are also some lessons that don't fall into one specific category but are still important and interesting, like addiction and intervention, community, leadership, and mental health, all through the experiences of different rock stars. They don't shy away from material that could be hard to discuss. For example, they provide a lesson for elementary schoolers on 9/11 through country music. They're also not afraid of controversy, providing plans for talking about things like cultural appropriation and the AIDS epidemic. Exploring the website allows teachers to filter by topic and grade level. Best of all, the resources are completely free. Not just to educators, but also to nerds and rock fans like myself—I must admit that while writing this chapter, I spent a solid few hours reading through the materials.

My dad had the opportunity to use some of their materials as a teacher and found them really engaging for the students. He's overseen the same materials being used by teachers in Lordstown where he served six years as Superintendent of Schools. They even have a social studies teacher who teaches History of Rock and Roll, which I think is awesome! He also brought people from the Foundation into a countywide professional development event that we have annually. It's called Innovative Day, and while I have to admit that I make fun of the name, I think it's awesome that so many teachers have been exposed to this material and can start using it in their classrooms.

Since we're such strong believers in the Foundation's work, we were thrilled to hear that a gala was being held in New York City to benefit the group. We immediately wanted to go, but it was being held at the Hard Rock Café after hours, so we weren't sure if I'd be able to get in. We've run into issues in the past—since I'm under 21, some venues are reluctant to let me in, though I don't drink and neither does my dad. So, my dad reached out to one of his contacts at the organization and asked. Not only did she say yes, but she invited us to come as the Foundation's guests. We immediately accepted and started planning a trip to New York.

New York is already one of my favorite places in the world. It combines everything I love: there's so much history, the literary landmarks, and, of course, Broadway! We've almost lost track by now of how many times we've been there, but we love it more and more every single time we go. I'll never forget the first trip—we were determined, in typical Armstrong fashion, to cram in as many of the iconic stops and tourist destinations as possible. We only had

12 hours in the city but that didn't stop us. We went to the top of the Empire State Building, walked the length of Central Park, and even made it down to Battery Park to see the Statue of Liberty. When we got back, I was telling my third-grade teacher about the trip, and she asked "Oh, wow, so how many days were you there?" "Twelve hours!" I answered.

We've been there many times since and we've never had a bad trip. We even got stuck there in the middle of Winter Storm Jonas in 2015, and it was completely crazy—public transportation was shut down and when we were outside, the piles of snow were higher than my head and we could barely see in front of use. Still we had an incredible time. Despite that insanity, the winter is absolutely one of my favorite time to be there. It always brings "Silver Bells," one of our favorite Christmas carols, to mind: "City sidewalks, busy sidewalks, dressed in holiday style…"

I was extremely excited to go not just for the benefit event but also because it was happening at the end of November. Our first draft of the book was almost finished—this was the last chapter that still needed to be written and the word count was getting progressively higher. I talked about going to the benefit all week as I was getting ready.

It was especially hilarious as I was packing to leave, wondering out loud what on earth I should be wearing to this gala. My roommate is a fashion major with a great sense of style, so she was offering her two cents, but I had to stop her and correct her—while I was grateful for her input, I knew she heard "gala" and thought "formal," but considering Stevie's hippie-pirate-gypsy-rocker look, I figured it wouldn't be quite on the level of black ties and gowns. I ended up going with a black button down shirt with one of my favorite social justice pins, that says "be a nice human," on the collar, along with black jeans, black boots, and my favorite black leather jacket from Florence.)

We had an extremely early flight out of Cleveland and landed in the city with enough of what we call "flex time" to have some fun before the event. We walked around for a while to see some of the iconic decorations in the city that had recently been put up and really started to feel in the Christmas spirit!

The Rockefeller Center ice rink and Bryant Park come alive at Christmas time even more than they normally do. We even ended up taking a photo in front of Radio City Music Hall, with its massive tree and glittering lights and garland, for our family Christmas card. We spent some time browsing in the Strand, a massive bookstore that we love.

My friend Nate, who I met in high school and now attends college in New Jersey, took the train in and we got to see a show together. Keeping with the rock theme of the weekend, it was *Jagged Little Pill*, a musical about contemporary issues set to Alanis Morisette's music. It's become our tradition that every time I'm in the city he'll take the train in and we'll see a show together. It's great because I've gotten to pass on my love of Broadway to another friend and keep in touch even though we're going to colleges that are states apart!

Afterwards, we grabbed some coffee—we were really starting to feel the effects of a flight that made us get up at 3 in the morning—and stopped briefly at our hotel to change before going over to the Hard Rock Café. We of course love Hard Rock Cafés—they're the perfect places for rock fans like us, full of history and cool artifacts. I've lost track of how many we've been to, but over the years we've gone in almost every city we've traveled to. We even ended up there in foreign countries. When I studied abroad in Italy, my dad and my grandparents came to visit over Thanksgiving break. We spent a few days in Florence, then went to Geneva, Switzerland and Paris, France.

Moira and Terry in Florence

Unfortunately, we'd picked a bad time to go to Paris. The country was in chaos because of the yellow vest protestors, who were taking to the streets because of an increase in fuel costs and other government actions. There were massive crowds of these protestors, plus swarms of police in response. Now, we're pretty savvy travelers and we've been fine in some sticky situations before, but as we were on a bus, the driver looked terrified that the crowd was going to tip his vehicle over, and the police were starting to tear gas the crowd. We knew we needed to get off the streets. Turning a corner, my dad pointed out a building in the distance where we knew we'd be safe: The Hard Rock Café! He jokes now that it's the closest thing we could've had to an American embassy.

My roommates, Leah and Maddy, also came to the Florence, Italy Hard Rock Café on one of our last nights in the city for drinks. We had a great time hanging out, talking about our favorite memories from the past few months, and, on my end, being horrified at how few of the artists on the walls they'd heard of. Luckily, though Times Square always seems chaotic, this time we were surrounded by people who were just as into the decor as we were!

At the door we met Christine. She is one of the awesome staff of TeachRock. After she checked us in, we browsed the restaurant area, enjoyed a buffet of delicious food, took in the silent auction with some cool items such as concert tickets and autographs, and put our names to a big card to sign for Stevie for his birthday. Rock music of course played while we snacked and watched a slideshow of quotes from teachers and students who took part in the TeachRock program.

The program started shortly after. Cleveland's own Drew Carey served as emcee, starting off the night with a live auction. There was a handwritten page of lyrics from Bono and two guitars signed by the entire E Street Band—between the three items, people in the audience donated over $250,000 to the foundation! We were amazed.

They then introduced several award winners of the night, including a teacher who uses the curriculum in her classroom, and played some videos from more teachers as well as famous supporters of the foundation. We heard from the head of the foundation, who discussed how it's being implemented, and the governor of New Jersey, who talked about the importance of the arts in education. He explained that New Jersey had an arts program in every single school district in the state, but that he wasn't satisfied with that—he wanted every state in America to have a record that strong of supporting students in the arts! We agreed. Then, Stevie himself came to the stage to talk about his program. He explained how rock gives students a voice and something to connect to, unlike other parts of the curriculum. He noted that this is an important way to keep kids engaged and in school who might not be otherwise, which helps fight the cycle of poverty and incarceration that continues when students drop out. He also called teachers "the last defense against ignorance" in the country, which we thought was an absolutely fantastic descriptor.

Of course, the night was also a celebration. Stevie's birthday had just passed, so the others brought balloons and a cake to the stage and we all sang to him, and then they launched into a concert featuring Southside Johnny and the Asbury Jukes. This New Jersey band is iconic, and we were so excited to see them again. We'd also been laughing all weekend because my dad told me a story about one of his friends who once saw them open for Bon Jovi. He was getting impatient wanting to see the main act and texted my dad annoyed that "this Johnny Jukebox guy won't get off the stage!" But we love Southside Johnny and we were thrilled to hear his hits, and it was cool to see special guests join throughout the night, including Gary US Bonds and, of course, Stevie himself—we certainly didn't expect him to stay in his seat all night!

Stevie tours with his band The Disciples of Soul. My Dad saw him at a TeachRock! event held at the Hard Rockscino in Richfield. They have a 21 and over rule so I could not attend. He told me many teachers were there as Stevie provides free tickets to their shows to teachers. My Dad was right when he said Stevie can lead a band! The night of the benefit, Stevie would

Terry's Take

I cannot say enough about TeachRock! During the pandemic, they made extra efforts to get their materials, all electronic and available for free, in the hands of teachers across the world. First class people and a first-class organization.

play with Southside Johnny and lead the house band through several party favorites.

We were exhausted by the time we left, but we found the energy to make one last stop in the city (other than the airport the next morning): John's Pizza. There's a lot of debate about the best pizza in NYC, but not for us. There's nothing better than John's, especially when you've just come from a rock concert. Thanks to Stevie and the entire staff at the foundation for all the work they do in supporting teachers and their students!

—Moira

Moira brings a bit of Cleveland to NYC with her iconic WMMS Buzzard t-shirt

OUTTAKES

Frankie Valli and the Four Seasons
December 2011 at Playhouse Square in Cleveland, Ohio

He was over eighty years old when we saw him, but his voice still reached those mind-blowingly high notes—and the crowds still went wild, including me. We gave him a standing ovation as he walked off the stage, and as he stopped to greet fans, I even got a handshake. As a musical buff as well, I also absolutely adore *Jersey Boys*. It was one of the first jukebox musicals to tell the story of a performer's life—although it's been followed up by some other incredible shows, like *The Cher Show* and *Ain't Too Proud.*   -*Terry*

THE WHO

May 15, 2015 at Nationwide Arena in Columbus, Ohio

We had the chance to see the third, at least alphabetically, of the Holy Trinity of British Rock and Roll when The Who came to Columbus, Ohio's Nationwide Arena. We had already seen the Rolling Stones, and if you count seeing Paul and Ringo both individually and together (at Ringo's induction into the Rock and Roll Hall of Fame), and now The Who, we've been fortunate to see them all!

The Who was one of the earliest bands I remember listening to. My parents had both albums and 8-track tapes of the band, and I listened to them as much as they did. I remember looking at the album cover for *Who by Numbers* and wanting to grab a pencil and complete the puzzle. I loved "Who are You," "Eminence Front," "You Better Bet"...the list goes on and on. I remember listening to them all in my room, sometimes with old-school headphones to not disturb my younger brother and sister.

Moira was excited to be seeing Rock and Roll royalty as well. It did not hurt when she found out who their opening act was. If you recall the letter "J" being one of the longest and most passionate in the book, you know Joan Jett has made quite an impression on our daughter!

Joan was great of course and gave way to Roger Daltrey and Pete Townshend taking the stage. Their presence was amazing, and it was like I was seeing them in their much younger days. The mannerisms, guitar licks, and Roger's ballet with the microphone transported me back to watching video concerts of them.

They had not missed a beat as they played all our favorites. Of course, "Baba O'Riley" cannot be played without talking about the generations of confusion about the title of the song. Moira reminds me that I likely told her dozens of times that the song is not called "Teenage Wasteland." She even repeated it herself; when in high school someone in her class saw her t-shirt from the concert and said, "I like their song 'Teenage Wasteland.' Ugh.

I laughed when she told me about it as she was not only prepared for such an exchange with the Rock and Roll uninitiated but one of my favorite television shows, *Freaks and Geeks*, had a similar exchange set in a high school. If you are reading this book, likely you yourself have had a similar exchange in your life.

My wife, as we have chronicled in the book, loves music and our passion for Classic Rock but she does not share the knowledge or love of it at our level. When we dated, I had first shared with her the song "Who are You." I was shocked to learn she had not heard it, so I was excited to share it with her. I was not one to curse much so she was also a bit shocked at a particular section of the lyrics. At the concert, I called our home phone to leave a little music on the voicemail, and I made sure it was The Who performing "Who are You" live, so that she could experience just a little of it with us. This is something we did at almost every concert we have attended... always picking a song that had personal meaning to us. Of course, this was before any of us had cell phones with good cameras...now we can take videos with much better quality.

One thing about The Who is that it is the favorite band for many in my generation (pun intended). Some of my best friends will quickly identify The Who as their favorite. My friend Mike took his son and we met up with them at the concert in Columbus. It was exciting for me as I had had his son in class when I was a teacher. He would also take me to see them a few years later when they stopped in Pittsburgh which was also a great show. Moira has a rule that I can't go without her if we have not seen them together, so Mike and I were good to go to that one.

While my job as Superintendent of Schools was very rewarding, I did miss the daily interactions with students in the classroom. I had the greatest kids which any educator will tell you makes it all worth it. As a school administrator we sometimes face situations where we advocate for kids in the face of adults who may not have the full story or may have a bias of some sort.

In one instance, I was trying to protect a student from being marginalized. A conversation with my friend John about the situation resonated with me and contains a bit of a mantra I often refer back to. A fan of Rock and Roll himself, he said to me," Terry, you are rock fan…just remember: the Kids are Alright."

The words of John and of The Who will forever ring in my ear with that.

—Terry

OUTTAKES

Joe Walsh
September 2015 at Packard Music Hall in Warren, Ohio

Moira has yet to see the Eagles, though Kim and I have, but seeing Joe Walsh live in our hometown of Warren, Ohio was as exciting as it gets. To make it more exciting it was kind of a homecoming for Joe Walsh, opening his tour with two nights in a row. At one time, he was a resident of Kent, where Kim and I graduated from college and where Moira currently attends. As we came into Packard Music Hall, there was a festival-type atmosphere with people tailgating.

While in town, he made an appearance at a local record store, the Record Connection, signing autographs and taking pictures with fans. This was something also done by Warren, Ohio native David Grohl (of Nirvana and Foo Fighters fame) when he was last in town.

Joe Walsh would play my favorite of his hits, "In the City." I love the song but Kim always brings up the fact it was in a movie that has some personal history for us. I worked the late shift at Sbarro's Pizza and would call Kim on the phone when I got home (pretty late typically). One night I called her when I got home and asked, "What are you doing?" She said, "There is this stupid movie on. It has some kind of baseball mime gang in it." I instantly responded with "It's *The Warriors*! I love that movie!" Of course I then immediately turned it on at my house. She did still marry me.

Not only was Joe Walsh as good on his own as with the Eagles, but his band that night was great as well. He shared memories of his time in Ohio and talked about the first time he played Packard with the James Gang. He even talked about the opening act they had, Mahoning Valley's own Glass Harp. It was a special and memorable night for us to see and hear him in Warren...hopefully for Mr. Walsh as well. *-Terry*

Terry in much younger days
working at Sbarro Pizza in the Eastwood Mall

THE X AMBASSADORS

November 5, 2019 at the House of Blues in Cleveland, Ohio

When we started working on this book, most of the letters of the alphabet weren't hard to assign to different bands that we'd seen through the years. In most cases, the hardest part was deciding which band we wanted to write about. There were a few exceptions, like the letter Q, but we figured out quickly which artists would fit into those missing letters. However we got stuck on X, and as we drove home from the airport on our first night of brainstorming, we actually ended up googling a list of bands and performers whose names start with X because we just could not think of anyone.

Unfortunately, that research didn't help that much. We hadn't heard of most of the bands we discovered and it was hard to imagine spending a night at a concert where we'd never heard a single one of their songs, and then writing about it in this book as passionately as we could write about someone like Joan Jett. Plus, some of the bands had broken up or weren't coming anywhere near us on their tour, so we felt like we might be stuck, and we were starting to get really worried about letter X.

Then my dad found that a band called the X Ambassadors would be coming to the House of Blues in Cleveland. The name sounded familiar, and when we looked them up on Spotify, their songs sounded familiar, so we bought tickets immediately.

The concert was taking place in mid-November, a few months after we first had the idea for the book. We'd been working on it throughout the summer, dividing up the letters based on which of us had a greater attachment to the band, and then working together on edits and additions. However, once the school year started, things became busy. My dad was working on it as his hobby to relax, between his Doctoral classes and work, and unfortunately, between my classes, job, internship, and trying to keep in touch with all of my friends both at school at back home, I had barely touched it at all since the semester began. However, when November rolled around, I thought of a solution.

Many writers know of November as National Novel Writing Month, a nonprofit program that encourages writers to finish a fifty-thousand-word draft of a novel in thirty days. Personally, I think it's a fantastic program that helps with the hardest part of writing: getting the words down on the paper. Perhaps ironically, I did it for the first time when I was in college studying abroad in Italy, which seems like the least likely time that someone would be able to finish a draft of a novel, but I got it done. I think it's a great program and the encouragement from professionals in the writing field are extremely helpful. So, though I wouldn't be starting totally from scratch with a blank slate on November 1, I decided that I would declare finishing a draft of this book as my project for National Novel Writing Month in 2019.

Unfortunately, November is also one of the most chaotic months of the year and the concert was also taking place on a Tuesday, which was my busiest day of the week. I ran from a meeting for my internship to a class to another class to work and then to a presentation for work. Throughout the day I was also doing some intense studying for an upcoming exam in my American history class. By the time my dad pulled up to my dorm to pick me up for the concert, I was completely exhausted but getting excited. I really needed a break and a concert was the perfect opportunity.

I also was glad to have a while in the car with my dad. We've always bonded over car rides and have several "long ways home" that allow us to keep talking and listening to music! Taking the long way also reminds us of the Supertramp song. Plus, our lives are so busy that we don't always have the chance to share everything that's going on over text or in person, so we got to catch up with everything, telling funny stories and listening to E Street Radio. We're a little addicted to Sirius Radio's music channels, from the interviews to the live concerts to just a great mix of music that we enjoy, from the general decade channels to specific channels devoted to artists we love. Doing their part in keeping classic rock alive are Sirius dee jays like Rachel Steele and Katherine Boyd (who broadcast from Cleveland at the Rock and Roll Hall of Fame), E Street Radio's Jim Rotolo and Dave Marsh (who is an awesome author too), and Classic Vinyl rockers Meg Griffin and Earle Bailey, as well as several Vee Jays from MTV like Alan Hunter, Mark Goodman, Cleveland native Nina Blackwood, and, for a while, Martha Quinn.

When we arrived at the House of Blues and headed into the lobby, we were super excited to be back in this very cool venue. In the lobby, there's a neat mural of Alan Freed—the radio host who coined the term "Rock and Roll" and organized the first rock concert—that always puts me in the mood to rock.

The evening began with two opening acts that night. We arrived partway through what we thought was the second. She was cool, but after she left the stage, another group that wasn't the X Ambassadors came onto the stage. My dad had had a really busy day too and we were both starving, so we decided that we would go down to the restaurant area for a bite to eat. We'd never actually gone there before and ended up asking a staff member for directions, because we knew the theatre part connected to the restaurant part but had never been there before. They directed us through a specific door, so that's where we went.

We were instantly suspicious because it seemed like we were going into the bowels of the building, into a place where we were not supposed to be. The feeling only intensified as we turned a corner and walked straight past the opening act that we had just seen leaving the stage!

However, we ran into another staff member who assured us that yes, we were heading in the right direction. We soon ended up in the restaurant. It had the same cool, artsy vibe as the theatre itself.

We had delicious food—my dad a burger and me a pulled pork sandwich—and continued talking. The restaurant was almost empty with just a few other guests so we sat there guessing why these other people were there. This table was a group of businessmen who were bored and walked over from their hotel. That table was a couple who visited the House of Blues in every new city they traveled to. And that one in the corner was a group of roadies who were waiting for their employers, the main act, just like we were.

"We could probably get away with telling the waiter that we work for the band, too," my dad whispered conspiratorially to me, pointing out the fact that both of us were dressed entirely in black. That, and we have a knack for blending in through the simple tactic of "walking with purpose and looking like we belong." Case in point: we're frequently mistaken for employees of the Rock and Roll Hall of Fame.

We didn't try to pretend that we worked for the X Ambassadors, but instead just enjoyed our dinner and then headed back upstairs. Our timing was perfect as we walked back into the theater just as the main act took the stage and the crowd went wild. It was really interesting and not what we expected as this is a newer band and we were anticipating more of a young crowd, but there was a huge range of ages and types of people there that night, all of whom appeared equally excited.

We saw people, from college-aged students like me to people who looked about my grandparents' age and everything in between, all of whom knew every word and were on their feet dancing. It was also a diverse crowd which was unusual—there's often a pretty large racial majority in the crowds at concerts we see. The O'Jays, for example, were a mostly African American crowd, whereas Styx and REO Speedwagon were almost entirely white men my dad's age. As we watched all of this happen, we wondered how had most of these people had gotten there. Were they just looking for a night out? Were the college students back at home because they had class the next morning? Were the two people in the row next to us, who didn't look remotely like music people but who hadn't sat down the entire night, the lead singer's parents or something?

When the music started, though, it didn't matter. The band was on their *Orion* tour, which was celebrating the release of their newest album of the same name, and they were clearly extremely excited. Their energy radiated off the stage and throughout the entire audience. Despite the small size of the venue, it felt like a stadium concert with the passion with which the band performed. The lead singer was dancing all over the place, as was the keyboardist, who I later learned was blind. I know that diversity in rock has come up a lot throughout the course of this book, but I'm going to get on my soapbox once again to say that it's not every day that you see someone in the rock and roll world that's disabled and is still an integral part of the band regardless. I was also thrilled to see a female bass player who doubled up on the keyboard and vocals at times.

We did end up leaving a little early because we were exhausted and we both had longer days ahead of us, but we had a great time anyway. Plus, I'd gotten to spend a fun night with my dad while forgetting about my stress for a while...and I'd discovered a new band that I genuinely really liked! For the next few days, as I walked and took buses around campus, I found myself queueing up the *Orion* album and the Spotify "This Is the X Ambassadors" playlist, bopping to the beat as I headed from class to class.

—Moira

Our X Ambassadors ticket stubs

WEIRD AL YANKOVIC

May 30, 2015 at Jacob's Pavilion in Cleveland, Ohio
June 24, 2016 at the Akron Civic Theatre in Akron, Ohio
July 6, 2019 at Playhouse Square in Cleveland, Ohio

Whenever I start a conversation with someone about music and they hear that I've seen over one hundred concerts, the inevitable next question is which ones have been my favorites. I have a few stock answers. Many of them have been covered in this book already. Our first time at the Rock Hall inductions. The second time we saw the Tallest Man on Earth. Pretty much any Bruce Springsteen concert. But there's always one response that surprises everyone, no matter how well they know me or how in-depth our conversations about music have become. Weird Al Yankovic. And don't laugh: he is genuinely fantastic.

We saw Weird Al for the first time in 2015. I don't remember why, but I was in somewhat of a bad mood that day and I didn't really want to be going to a concert at all. I just wanted to bury myself in a book for a few hours and go to bed. But we drove up to Cleveland regardless. I knew that concerts typically put me in a better mood, but I had no idea just how much of a 180 my mood was about to take. It's impossible to be unhappy at a Weird Al concert.

First, the rest of the crowd is incredibly passionate. I was nowhere near that level of knowledge about his career and music and I had no idea that there would be people there in full costume who knew every word! It was even intergenerational. I saw all ages, from grandparents to literal babies, and it was adorable watching a set of parents in front of me dancing and singing "Dare to Be Stupid" to their tiny child. It was a friendly, cheerful atmosphere that was so enjoyable to be a part of.

And Al himself is just so unpredictable. I know the drill now, three concerts later, but there were costume changes both for him and his entire band, video clips and accompaniment, and a stage entrance via Segway during "White and Nerdy." The concert was at Jacob's Pavilion, a cool quasi-outdoor venue on the Cuyahoga River, and we were convinced that he might jump off one of the boats floating by with a wedding party!

I was familiar with some of the songs just from pop culture, and genuinely enjoy them—they're not just parodies, they're truly witty and intelligent, too. I also found that, while I'm not a huge fan of most modern music, I can live with adaptations that are based around polka! There are also quite a few that appeal to my own personal pet peeves. As an English major (or future English major at the time), I was obsessed with "Word Crimes," a Blurred Lines cover that disparages all the English language's most common grammar mistakes.

I didn't even realize that it was a Blurred Lines cover until college—literally, three years later, standing in the line at one of the dining halls. The song came on the radio and I told my roommate that it sounded so familiar, but I just couldn't place it. She suggested that I might've heard it on the radio before, heard it in a commercial or on TV—then it clicked. It was a Weird Al song. I'd just never heard the original before.

We immediately decided that we wanted to take my mom to see him too. I think she was a little suspicious at first. Like we've mentioned, she doesn't have the same taste in music as we do, and I don't think she believed that Weird Al could possibly be as good as we were saying! But she humored us, and we ended up again having a fantastic time. This time, we were at another very interesting venue. The Akron Civic Theater, in downtown Akron, was originally built in 1929 modeled after a Moorish castle with a Mediterranean theme, including medieval carvings, European antiques, and Italian alabaster sculptures. It's also an atmospheric theatre, meaning that the ceiling is designed to look like the sky, with embedded stars that actually twinkle and clouds that meander across the horizon as you watch from your seat. We found it a little off-putting at first, because while it's beautiful, it can be a little distracting. However, it's the perfect venue for Weird Al. It's unique and it takes some getting used to, but at the end of the day, it's undeniably cool.

Of course, not everyone is convinced of this. We were seated behind two guys who had come to the concert together and were chatting before the show.

"You know," one said. "My wife never wants to come to these concerts."

"Yeah," the other echoed. "I don't understand why, but she just doesn't get Weird Al."

My mom, meanwhile, was holding back laughter. "I understand why." she whispered to my dad and I.

Al also has some very famous fans. As a musical aficionado and a history major, I absolutely love *Hamilton*, as does my dad. He's always referred to him as his "favorite framer of the Constitution" and when he was a teacher, he would ask students who

Kim's Commentary

When Terry and Moira wanted me to go see Weird Al with them, oh yes, I had my doubts. They are pretty good scouts though and it was a great show.

their favorite framer was, too. We were both extremely excited— although when I first told him that the musical was being made, he thought I was making it up so that he'd take me to New York! But I was very lucky that, thanks to both of us being total nerds, we got on the *Hamilton* bandwagon early and were able to see it on Broadway with the original cast. We also happened to go to BroadwayCon around the same time and see a panel of the cast, including Lin Manuel Miranda, and were absolutely blown away. He's a genius and we were so impressed by everything he had to say about both the process and the history behind the musical. So, we were thrilled, of course, to see him partner with Weird Al on the Hamilton Polka. I remember the first time I heard it, watching Lin and Al lip-synch to it on a late-night show, and then humming it for the rest of the day.

He's also connected to some other famous fandoms, most notably, Star Wars. He has a few songs that are about the movie series that he usually plays at the end of his shows. I must be honest: I am not a Star Wars fan. I don't think I'd seen a single one of the movies until high school, when we had to watch the first one for an assignment in English class to learn about the hero's journey. And even after that, I had absolutely no desire to see any of the others. Perhaps the case in point here is that when my mythology/sci fi elective decided to go to the movies to see the newest one when it was released my senior year, I actually fell asleep.

However, I'll be right there next to the hard-core Star Wars fans, pulling up the flashlight on my phone so I can wave it back and forth as I sing along to "The Saga Begins"—"my, my, this here Anakin guy, may be Vader someday later, now he's just a small fry, and he left his home and kissed his mommy goodbye saying soon I'm gonna be a Jedi"—because for those few minutes, we're all Star Wars people.

When we heard, in 2019, that Al was going on another tour, this one called "No Strings Attached" and accompanied by an orchestra, we knew we had to go. We were back at one of our all-time favorite venues for this, although we're typically there for theatre—Playhouse Square.

We have already shared our family love of theater and Playhouse Square. Not only the second largest theater district in the United States and a vibrant arts and culture scene but also a historical theater district with many of today's top Broadway and Hollywood stars having taken part in productions throughout its history.

One such actor, and also a family favorite, is Tom Hanks. I still remember my dad telling me he was a fan all the way back to his sitcom days (Bosom Buddies and memorable guest star on Family Ties). What surprises some is that one of his first paid acting gigs was in Cleveland as part of the Great Lakes Theater company.

We were excited to find out that Tom Hanks would be taking part in a fundraiser for the Cleveland Film Commission. We got tickets and counted down the days not knowing what the fundraiser would be like. As we entered the venue, we were greeted by a nice couple who asked "Do you know Tom?" Of course, we answered we did not and asked if they did. They did and went on to explain that when he is in town, he gathers his old friends from the Great Lakes Theater company together for an intimate reunion. This cemented him in our minds as a truly great guy.

While we would not be attending the intimate reunion that would follow, we did get to see and hear Mr. Hanks give remarks to those attending the reunion. A story we will not soon forget that he told was when he was working as a paid actor in Cleveland, he would spend the offseason in New York trying to make it. He would receive unemployment checks from Ohio and would cash them in Cleveland. Through a rather serendipitous turn he shared with everyone that the bank he would cash the check at in New York is now where the Bubba Gump Shrimp Company restaurant is now located. We could not wait to share that story with our waiter the next time we went to New York.

The tour that Weird Al was on also had a movie theme to it as they played classic opening themes of several famous movies, from *Jurassic Park* to *Star Wars*. They were fantastic—but they played for such a long time that I leaned over to my dad and whispered, "Do you think he did this just to trick his audiences into listening to an orchestral concert?" Certainly not a bad thing, and something that I could see Al doing.

He soon came out and performed all of the hits. The interspersed videos provided an additional highlight. Throughout the night, we get to see footage from music videos throughout Al's career, which for me is particularly fun because I wasn't around during much of his career itself.

There's also always a lot of humor involved. At the last concert, I remember Al telling us all that he had a brand-new song to play. He'd been working on it for a while and he was really proud of how it turned out. He wasn't sure how we'd like it, but he wanted to share it with us anyway. He stepped up to the mic, and he sang approximately thirty seconds of a song called "Harvey the Wonder Hamster." It was one of my favorite moments of the night. There's also the satirical song for "Weasel Stomping Day," which everyone sings along with as eagerly as they would for Christmas carols.

Al's backup band—not the orchestra, but the band itself—are also fantastic. They seem to be great sports, making the same costume changes as Al himself, like when the entire band dresses as the members of Devo or in full surgeon gear. And probably my top favorite moment of the night, no matter how many times I see him in concert, is a song that's usually one of the last of the night as well. "Amish Paradise." It always makes me think of my dad, who assigned a project when he was a teacher called "Sociology Rocks" combining music and politics. One student in a rural district did his on "Amish Paradise" and actually did a photoshoot for the album cover in a field! Everyone onstage puts on full beards, tall hats, and black cloaks, and there's a projection of a candlelit choir behind them, providing virtual backup, looking almost spooky as they're lit from below with the flames. And the haunting chorus is balanced perfectly by how hilarious the lyrics are.

It's a totally different kind of concert experience from the others I usually like—it's funny rather than emotional—but it's incredible regardless and I could see him a thousand times without ever getting bored.

—Moira

ZZ Top

**October 3, 2015 at Cambria County War Memorial Arena
in Johnstown, Pennsylvania**

Terry with ZZ Top Eliminator car at the Rock and Roll Hall of Fame

Though the letter Z is limited I cannot imagine picking anyone other than ZZ Top. They have had the same line up from the beginning and continue to tour year after year...and are the kings of irony as the only guy without the famous beard has the last name of Beard (Frank Beard)!

I remember watching them on MTV when it burst on the scene. "Sharp Dressed Man," "Legs" and "Gimme All Your Lovin" seemed to be played on their rotation all the time...and my friends and I were all fine with it. I remember thinking as I watched the videos, is it possible these ladies would roll up in that awesome car to the car wash I was working at and whisk me away? We all know the answer to that but who did not have similar questions?

Once we were into high school, their songs were still popular. I recall a high school skit session during our spirit week that featured three teachers coming out to do lip sync to "Sharp Dressed Man" but changing the words to "Well Dressed Man." I still am not sure why they changed the one word, but ZZ Top's presence in culture was huge.

My family was not a big county fair family, but I recall one time my dad took my sister, brother, and I to the fair. Two things stand out. We talked him into going into one of those tourist-trap deals where there is a Human/spider and bearded lady. When we were in there, a guy had a bed of nails and said he wanted the biggest guy in the room to come up. Mostly due to not many people being in the room my dad was the biggest person in the room. The guy asked my dad to touch the nails on a bed of nails. My Dad did and confirmed the authenticity of the nails to the "crowd" He then proceeded to lay down on the nails and invited my dad to stand on his chest. Reluctantly my dad did so and within a second or two the guy was yelling "Get off, Get off." It was hilarious.

The second fair memory I have is of playing a game and winning a ZZ Top mirror. I was proud of my mirror and took it over to my grandparents with me one weekend. My Grandpa asked, "Who is Easy Top?" Love that guy...he really wanted to know despite getting the name wrong. He was the same guy who stood in line in an attempt to take me to a Kiss concert.

I can't recall how I got one, but I had one of the ZZ Top keychains just like in the video. I loved that keychain. It had sat

Terry shows off his ZZ Top mirror while brother Jason displays his Care Bears

in my room, whether living with my parents, out on my own, and even newly married, when one of my friends at work bought a new car. He showed me the car one day after work. It was when the PT Cruiser was new and all the rage. You could see the excitement on his face. One of the things we had in common, despite him actually being older than my dad, was a love for ZZ Top. I went home that day and grabbed the keychain and took it to work the next day to give it to him to go along with his new car. I was happy to do this for a friend, though later I did replace that ZZ Top keychain with another.

We've also brought ZZ Top into one of our favorite family traditions. Every Halloween, our family picks a different theme and we all dress to that theme. We've been characters from many Disney movies and favorite book series, but one year we decided to all dress as favorite Rock and Roll Hall of Fame inductees. Moira was Johnny Cash, Kim was Cyndi Lauper, and I was one of the members of ZZ Top, complete with beard and a new keychain!

The concert took place in Johnstown, Pennsylvania at the Cambria County War Memorial Arena. This was the only time we have visited this venue. Warren, Ohio is located in Northeast Ohio and very close to the western Pennsylvania border. We would often venture across the state line not only to attend concerts and other events in Pittsburgh but a little town called Sharon, Pennsylvania had a store called Kraynacks that had a Christmasland inside that many in the Mahoning Valley would trek to annually. My wife and I even got engaged there when I proposed in front of a tree we really liked. We honeymooned in nearby Clark, PA at the southern-inspired Tara Country Inn.

Johnstown was not a town I had ventured to, about a two-and-a-half-hour drive from Warren, but seeing ZZ Top well worth it. When I bought tickets to the concert, I recalled reading about the terrible flood that destroyed much of the town. As we drove there I was reminded of the geographical and cultural differences between western PA (Pittsburgh) and eastern PA (Philadelphia) and the long stretch of the middle. I have heard it referred in politics by James Carville as something like "Pittsburgh, Philadelphia and Alabama in the middle." Not too far off when you drive between the two cities, but it is not without sites that we as a family have visited.

Of course we have taken in Pittsburgh for concerts, shows and sporting events (Pirates and Penguins—not the Steelers!) and Philadelphia when Moira was visiting Swarthmore on a college visit—we took in the historic Constitution Hall, the Liberty Bell, and other historical sites and of course the Rocky statue. I ran up the steps, though we took a photo of Moira sprawled out on the steps looking like she collapsed. A lesser known site in eastern Pennsylvania that was one of our favorite family vacations was a Sesame Street-themed park in Langhorn, Pennsylvania called Sesame Place—one of the best vacations we ever had.

We got into town early, checked out a town building that had a historical display about the floods, and then visited a modern Holiday Inn. The rural area was nice and the people too, but Moira and I missed the *city* that we typically visited when we went to a concert. My wife is right...Moira and I are city folk.

The arena was smaller than the large city venues but that made for an experience where truly there was not a bad seat in the house. The opening act was not one of our favorites and reminded us how lucky we were when we have seen great opening acts. It also made the crowd even more anxious to see the little ol' band from Texas.

ZZ Top has been a band since before I was even born, but you would never know it. They rocked the crowd with all of their hits. Young and old and in-between, everyone in the crowd sang along and even played a little air guitar. It was obvious there were many in the crowd that have seen them many times before and even follow them from town to town. Beyond their hits they just know how to rock...and you knew they were having as much fun as those of us in the crowd.

A ZZ Top concert is a good example of how Rock and Roll brings people from different backgrounds to a common culture. My wife always calls me a bit too button down and points out that I only have one pair of blue jeans. We rocked along with many in motorcycle leather and enjoyed each other's company all through night, united like those from different backgrounds that share the love of a sports team.

—Terry

ENCORE

*Moira and Terry at Rock and Roll Forever Foundation Gala
to honor Stevie Van Zandt*

Just because the alphabet is over doesn't mean we're done! Like any good rock concert finishes out with an encore, we have one last portion to our book. We have seen so many incredible concerts, but we have also lost many rockers too soon and we wanted to pay tribute to them as well.

It's probably very clear that having seen Bruce Springsteen and the E Street Band multiple times, they're one of our favorites, partially because there are always so many powerful moments over the (four-hour) course of a concert. One of those that gets us every time is "Tenth Avenue Freeze-Out." Bruce always talks about Clarence Clemons and how even though he passed way too soon, his spirit is with us. Not only does this apply to Clarence, he says, but also to all the others that people in the venue have lost. All of them are with us as music brings us together. From the in-memoriam sections of the Rock Hall inductions to the knowledge that someone is gone when you put on one of their records, we feel this all the time.

Listing all of those people for us could be a book of its own, so we won't go into too much detail, but many of them deserve a mention.

In the most recent past, we've lost Tom Petty, David Bowie, Prince, and Eddie Money. These were particularly hard as we had the chance to see them and missed that chance. These kinds of deaths remind us every day that we should seize the moment. Not every rock star will be around forever, and we want to take every chance we have to see them before they're gone.

There are also many older artists who passed away long before Moira was even born but that we would have loved to have seen. Elvis Pressley, Johnny Cash, Jimi Hendrix, Janis Joplin, and the other two Beatles are probably the biggest examples. These were musical giants, many of whom were lost too soon. We would have loved to have seen them, and many others, before the world lost them, but we know we will always have their music...and the memories others share with us! Talking to older rock fans who have been around long enough to see some of those people is one of Moira's absolute favorite things to do, and I also love that aspect of social media. So many of the people Moira follows on Twitter and Instagram post old photos and memories of bands Moira know as older, from their younger days.

We also, of course, still have many performers on our rock concert bucket list. Moira missed out on the Eagles (though it's true, she did record an album) and though Kim and Terry did see Phil Collins, Moira still has him on the list. The list is endless but includes Billy Squier, Cat Stevens, Van Morrison, the Village People, Tom Morello, the Pretenders, Bad Company, the Dropkick Murphys, and the Foo Fighters (which is particularly ironic considering Dave Grohl is from our hometown and we've spent some time in the alley downtown dedicated to him)! We also take pride in the fact of Cleveland as the home to the Rock and Roll Hall of Fame—just an hour drive from home towards the North coast and we can live amongst our Rock and Roll heroes!

As we "worked" on writing this book together like everyone else we ran into the pandemic brought on by Covid-19 throughout 2020-2021. We were sad that we could not see our favorite bands but much more concerned about the impact it was having on families that dealt with the virus and those put out of work by the virus. We tried to do our small part by supporting fundraisers including some put on by classic rockers as well as organizations such as Save our Stages and TeachRock.

Moira at Dave Grohl Alley

We took precautions like everyone else, but cannot wait until the pandemic is all behind us and we are back out there seeing and supporting our favorites bands. Our family did not incur the costs of travel ball sports teams, we drive cars that reach 150,000 miles, and like others look for deals everywhere we can (The Armstrong family motto is: If it's free, it's for me). This has all helped give us the ability to have so many special moments as a family.

Now this is the point at which the rest of the band would take a bow before leaving the stage, so it's an appropriate time for us to thank the people who made it possible for us to get here. A full list would be endless, but we're going to do our best to acknowledge everyone who has supported, inspired, and rocked with us throughout these experiences. As a special nod to all the people in our lives who love music as much as we do, we've included their first concerts in parentheses after their names!

We would both like to thank our family for their support: Kim/Mom (The Beach Boys), Terry's mom Debbie (George Michael), Terry's dad Ken (REO Speedwagon), brother Jason (Nine Inch Nails/David Bowie), and sister Jennifer (George Michael) and her husband Travis (Donnie Iris and the Cruisers), and Kim's mom Polly (Beach Boys), Kim's dad Randy (Led Zeppelin), and sister Donna (Kiss) and her husband Norman (Stevie Wonder/Earth, Wind, and Fire).

We are also both incredibly grateful to the bands we've been able to see and all of their hard work to become the performers they are, the many behind the scenes staffers who have made our experiences at concerts even better, the Rock and Roll Hall of Fame and its incredible staff (from CEO Greg Harris, to Jason Hanley who, through his role as Vice President of Education and Visitor Engagement, early on engaged Terry's students as part of the Rockin in the Schools program, to Lauren Onkey who engaged teachers as part of the Rock Hall's Teacher Summer Institute when Terry attended, and everyone on Team Rock Hall) for everything they do to make it the best location in the nation.

Thanks also goes out to all of the authors and music journalists who have written about rock and roll before us. Your work entertained, educated and inspired us. Thanks also to those dee jays who rocked and entertained so many of us. The list is endless but to name just a few: Cleveland's WMMS alum Jeff and Flash, Youngstown's WSRD/WHOT alum Thomas John, Youngstown's Y103 alum Lynn Davis, CD106/93.3 alums Fast Freddie Woak and Casey Malone, Youngstown's WHOT AC and Kelly, Cleveland's 97.5 WONE's Tim Daugherty, the Rock and Roll Authority, the legendary Norm Nite, and iconic WMMS alum and current Sirius Underground Garage program director Kid Leo.

Terry would like to thank his friends Bill Boscheff (White Snake/Quiet Riot), John Britton (Richie Havens/Bruce Springsteen), Arlo Brookhart (Jimmy Buffett), Mike Chaffee (Jackson Browne), Brent Currington (Billy Joel), David Folsom (Stone Temple Pilots), Michelle Folsom-Petiya (Captain & Tenille), Mark Garramone (Wild Horses), John Gilanyi (Joe Walsh), Randy Hafner (Huey Lewis and the News), Steve Haynie (Kenny Rogers), Brian Hiland (Tina Turner), Pat Hogan (Gordon Lightfoot), Rob Hollada (Alabama), Frank Konopka (Donnie Iris and the Cruisers), Matt Kresic (Lionel Richie/Tina Turner), Bob Kujala (Dink), Mark Lichnerowicz (Van Halen/BTO) Darcy Lichnerowicz (Steve Green) Pete Lucic/Preston Steele (Kiss), Brent Milhoan (Prince), Jim Phillips (Left End), Phil

Vigorito (Alice Cooper), and Rich Zigarovich (Kiss).

Moira would like to thank the teachers and librarians who have sparked their love of reading and writing over the years and later became friends: Cindy Baer (Yes), Amanda Daquelente (The Beach Boys), Lori Faust (John Denver), Gary Lendak (The Cars), and Thom Williams (Journey/Heart). Moira would also like to thank all of the friends who have been part of these memories, especially Jordan George (Macklemore), who was Moira's long-suffering roommate during the drafting of this book (and several others).

We would like to thank those that read our book and offered such nice reviews and words of encouragement: Kent State University History Professor Ken Bindas, who taught some of our favorite classses (The Ohio Players); Author and Media contributor Capri Cafaro (The Beach Boys); Executive Director of Trumbull County Tourism (Ohio), Beth Kotwis-Carmichael (The Michael Stanley Band); Actor John Dossett (Cat Stevens); *Tribune Chronicle/Youngstown Vindicator* Entertainment Editor Andy Gray (Rush/Uriah Heap/Judas Priest); Author Garin Pirnia (Huey Lewis and the News); Diversity and Inclusion Consultant Aaron Stubbs, a former student of Terry's, helping represent all the students Terry had during his years of teaching that mean so much to him (George Clinton and the Parliament Funkadelic); and Activist/Free Speech Pioneer Mary Beth Tinker (Janis Joplin/Al Green).

Lastly, we want to thank our editor Ryan Forsythe (Kiss/Ted Nugent) for making our story better (and for having so many shared interests)! We wouldn't got to this point without you.

This may be the end of our alphabetical journey and our book, but as classic rock fans know, we will never let Rock and Roll die. No matter who we are, we all join together cheering on our favorite rock legends, strumming our air guitars in the crowd (and in the car when we think no one is looking), throwing up the one-armed fist pump, and joining the fight to make sure that rock and roll lives forever. We're so glad to have been on this long, strange trip (pun intended) together and we're looking forward to many more years of music and the memories to come. So, there's just one more thing to say, in the words of the great Chuck Berry: hail, hail Rock and Roll!

—Terry and Moira

THE DRIVE HOME

For the Record:
An Appendix of All the Concerts
Attended by Moira and/or Terry

Band Name, Date, *Venue,* Who attended
[Notes]

AC/DC, 9/2016, *Nationwide Arena in Columbus, Ohio,* Terry and Moira

Adams, Bryan, 8/2019, *DTE Energy Center in Clarkston, Michigan,* Terry and Moira

Adams, Richard Todd, 4/2015, *Packard Music Hall in Warren, Ohio,* Terry, Kim and Moira [Neil Berg's 100 Years of Broadway]

Aerosmith, 8/2015, *Tom Benson Stadium at the Football Hall of Fame in Canton, Ohio,* Terry and Moira [Football Hall of Fame Ceremony Festival]

Air Supply, 10/2015, *Disney Epcot Center in Orlando, Florida,* Terry, Rob, Moira, Andrew and Rachel [Eat to the Beat concert series]

Alabama, 8/2013, *Playhouse Square in Cleveland, Ohio,* Terry, Kim and Moira

Allen, David, 8/2013, *St. George Theatre in Memphis, Tennessee,* Terry and Moira [International Elvis Tribute Competition]

America, 7/2014, *Ohio State Fairgrounds-Celeste Center in Columbus, Ohio,* Terry and Moira

Aron, Jesse, 8/2013, *St. George Theatre in Memphis, Tennessee,* Terry and Moira [International Elvis Tribute Competition]

Association, The, 9/2015, *Canfield Fairgrounds in Canfield, Ohio,* Terry,
Moira and Brittany [Happy Together Tour]

Awolnation, 6/2015, *Heinz Field in Pittsburgh, PA,* Terry and Moira

Bachman Turner Overdrive, 7/2014, *Ohio State Fairgrounds-Celeste Center in Columbus, Ohio,* Terry and Moira

Bachman, Randy of Guess Who and BTO, 3/2015, *Quicken Loans Arena in Cleveland, Ohio,* Terry, Moira and Antiggonie [Moondog Coronation Ball]

Barnett, Mandy, 12/2012, *Packard Music Hall in Warren, Ohio,* Terry and Moira

Barrone, Jim, 8/2013, *St. George Theatre in Memphis, Tennessee,* Terry and Moira [International Elvis Tribute Competition]; 8/2013, *St. George Theatre,* Terry and Moira [International Elvis Tribute Competition final]

Baseball Project, The, 7/2019, *Rock and Roll Hall of Fame in Cleveland, Ohio,* Terry and Moira [Baseball All Star Game Event]

Beach Boys, The, 9/1984, *Canfield Fairgrounds in Canfield, Ohio,* Kim and Pigott Family; 7/2011, *DTE Energy Center in Clarkston, Michigan,* Terry, Kim and Moira; 10/2015, *Packard Music Hall in Warren, Ohio,* Terry, Kim, Moira and Adam; 7/2014 **(with John Stamos),** *Ohio State Fairgrounds-Celeste Center in Columbus, Ohio,* Terry, Kim and Moira

Benatar, Pat with Neil Giraldo, 6/2016, *Heinz Hall in Pittsburgh, PA,* Terry and Moira

Bill Cherry, 2/2012, *Lima Civic Center in Lima, Ohio,* Terry and Moira [One of Elvis Tribute Artists (Elvis Lives)]

Black Wolf and the Thief, 6/2017, *Mocha House in Warren, Ohio,* Terry and Moira; 7/2017, *Front Porch Winery in Trumbull County, Ohio,* Terry and Moira; 6/2018, *Enzos Banquet Hall in Warren, Ohio,* Terry, Kim, Moira and guests [Moira's Graduation party]

Blackwood Quartet, The, 1/2014, *Playhouse Square in Cleveland, Ohio,* Terry and Moira

Blondie, 6/2015, *Packard Music Hall in Warren, Ohio,* Terry, Kim and Moira

Blue Oyster Cult, 7/2014, *Ohio State Fairgrounds-Celeste Center in Columbus, Ohio,* Terry and Moira

Bon Jovi, Jon, 3/2017, *Quicken Loans Arena in Cleveland, Ohio,* Terry, Rob Hollada and Stephanie; 1/2020, *Madison Square Garden in New York City,* Terry and Moira [Guest during the concert of Billy Joel]

Bonham, Greg, 10/2012, *Packard Music Hall in Warren, Ohio,* Moira, Nan and Pa

Bonham, Jason (Led Zeppelin Experience), 7/2017, *Giant Center in Hershey, PA,* Terry and Moira

Booth Brothers, The, 9/2012, *KFEC Expo Center in Louisville, Kentucky,* Moira, Nan and Pa [National Quartet Convention]; 9/2013, *KFEC Expo Center,* Moira, Nan and Pa [National Quartet Convention]

Boston, 8/2012, *Ohio State Fairgrounds Celeste Center in Columbus, Ohio,* Terry and Moira

Bowlings, The, 9/2013, *KFEC Expo Center in Louisville, Kentucky,* Moira, Nan and Pa [National Quartet Convention]

Brooks, Garth, 10/2015, *Quicken Loans Arena in Cleveland, Ohio,* Terry, Kim and Moira

Browders, The, 3/2011, *Westfall High School in Williamsport, Ohio,* Moira, Nan and Pa [Westfall Gospel Sing]; 3/2012, *Westfall High School,* Moira, Nan and Pa [Westfall Gospel Sing]

Browns, The, 9/2013, *KFEC Expo Center in Louisville, Kentucky,* Moira, Nan and Pa [National Quartet Convention]

Browne, Jackson, 6/2016, *Akron Civic Theater in Akron, Ohio,* Terry and Moira

Buckinghams, The, 9/2015, *Canfield Fairgrounds in Canfield, Ohio,* Terry, Moira and Brittany [Happy Together Tour]

Butterfield, Paul and the Blues Band, 4/2015, *Public Hall in Cleveland, Ohio,* Terry and Moira [Rock and Roll Hall of Fame Ceremony]

Canton Junction, 9/2013, *KFEC Expo Center in Louisville, Kentucky,* Moira, Nan and Pa [National Quartet Convention]

Carbone, Anthony, 8/2013, *St. George Theatre in Memphis, Tennessee,* Terry and Moira [International Elvis Tribute Competition]

Carter, Carlene, 1/2015, *Playhouse Square in Cleveland, Ohio,* Terry, Kim and Moira

Cass, Irv, 8/2013, *St. George Theatre in Memphis, Tennessee,* Terry and Moira [International Elvis Tribute Competition]

Chambliss, Michael, 8/2013, *St. George Theatre in Memphis, Tennessee,* Terry and Moira [International Elvis Tribute Competition]; 8/2013, *St. George Theatre,* Terry and Moira [International Elvis Tribute Competition final]

Charlotte Richie, 9/2011, *Covelli Center in Youngstown, Ohio,* Moira, Nan and Pa [Gaither Homecoming Tour]

Cheap Trick, 8/2015, *Ohio State Fairgrounds Celeste Center in Columbus, Ohio,* Terry and Moira; 7/2016, *Riverbend Music*

Center in Cincinnati, Ohio, Terry and Moira; 7/2017, *Giant Center in Hershey, PA,* Terry and Moira

Cher, 5/2014, *Quicken Loans Arena in Cleveland, Ohio,* Terry, Kim and Moira

Chicago, 2/2016, *Packard Music Hall in Warren, Ohio,* Terry and Moira

Childs, Andy, 8/2013, *Memphis Tennessee,* Terry and Moira [Part of Elvis Week]

Chuck Wagon Gang, The, 9/2012, *KFEC Expo Center in Louisville, Kentucky,* Moira, Nan and Pa [National Quartet Convention]

Clayton, Lawrence, 4/2015, *Packard Music Hall in Warren, Ohio,* Terry, Kim and Moira [Neil Berg's 100 Years of Broadway]

Cleveland Orchestra, 8/2010, *Blossom Music Center in Cuyahoga Falls, Ohio,* Terry, Kim, Moira, Donna, Norman, Nan and Pa

Coasters, Cornell Gunther's, 9/2012, *Packard Music Hall in Warren, Ohio,* Terry, Kim and Moira

Collingsworth Family, The, 9/2012, *KFEC Expo Center in Louisville, Kentucky,* Moira, Nan and Pa [National Quartet Convention]; 9/2013, *KFEC Expo Center,* Moira, Nan and Pa [National Quartet Convention]

Collins, Chad, 8/2013, *St. George Theatre in Memphis, Tennessee,* Terry and Moira [International Elvis Tribute Competition]; 8/2013, *St. George Theatre,* Terry and Moira [International Elvis Tribute Competition final]

Cooper, Alice, 5/2016, *Packard Music Hall in Warren, Ohio,* Terry and Moira

Cordell, Matt, 8/2013, *St. George Theatre in Memphis, Tennessee,* Terry and Moira [International Elvis Tribute Competition]; 8/2013, *St. George Theatre,* Terry and Moira [International Elvis Tribute Competition final]

Costello, Elvis, 7/2015, *Blossom Music Center in Cuyahoga Falls, Ohio,* Terry and Moira

Cowsills, The, 9/2015, *Canfield Fairgrounds in Canfield, Ohio,* Terry, Moira and Brittany [Happy Together Tour]

Crabb, Jason, 9/2012, *KFEC Expo Center in Louisville, Kentucky,* Moira, Nan and Pa [National Quartet Convention]

Creedence Clearwater Revisited, 4/2012, *Quicken Loans Arena in Cleveland, Ohio,* Terry and Moira [Moondog Coronation Ball]; 11/2013, *Stambaugh Auditorium in Youngstown, Ohio,* Terry, Kim and Moira

Crist Family, The, 9/2012, *KFEC Expo Center in Louisville, Kentucky,* Moira, Nan and Pa [National Quartet Convention]; 9/2013, *KFEC Expo Center,* Moira, Nan and Pa [National Quartet Convention]

Cropper, Steve, 4/2015, *Public Hall in Cleveland, Ohio,* Terry and Moira [Rock and Roll Hall of Fame Ceremony]

Cullipher, Michael, 8/2013, *St. George Theatre in Memphis, Tennessee,* Terry and Moira [International Elvis Tribute Competition]

Cyrus, Miley, 4/2015, *Public Hall in Cleveland, Ohio,* Terry and Moira [Rock and Roll Hall of Fame Ceremony]

Dalton Gang, The, 3/2011, *Westfall High School in Williamsport, Ohio,* Moira, Nan and Pa [Westfall Gospel Sing]; 3/2012, *Westfall High School,* Moira, Nan and Pa [Westfall Gospel Sing]

David Phelps, 9/2011, *Covelli Center in Youngstown, Ohio,* Moira, Nan and Pa [Gaither Homecoming Tour]

Dean Z, 8/2013, *St. George Theatre in Memphis, Tennessee,* Terry and Moira [International Elvis Tribute Competition]; 8/2013, *St. George Theatre,* Terry and Moira [International Elvis Tribute Competition final]; 1/2018, *Playhouse Square in Cleveland, Ohio,* Terry and Moira [Elvis Birthday Tribute]

Def Leppard, 8/2014, *Blossom Music Center in Cuyahoga Falls, Ohio,* Terry and Moira

Diamond, Neil, 7/2012, *Quicken Loans Arena in Cleveland, Ohio,* Terry and Moira; 3/2015, *Schottenstein Center in Columbus, Ohio,* Terry and Moira; 5/2017, *Quicken Loans Arena,* Terry, Kim and Moira

Diamonds, The, 9/2011, *Packard Music Hall in Warren, Ohio,* Terry, Kim and Moira

Diplomats, The, 9/2012, *KFEC Expo Center in Louisville, Kentucky,* Moira, Nan and Pa [National Quartet Convention]

Dixie Echoes, The, 9/2012, *KFEC Expo Center in Louisville, Kentucky,* Moira, Nan and Pa [National Quartet Convention]

Dixie Melody Blues, The, 9/2012, *KFEC Expo Center in Louisville, Kentucky,* Moira, Nan and Pa [National Quartet Convention]

Dolenz, Mickey of the Monkees, 4/2012, *Quicken Loans Arena in Cleveland, Ohio,* Terry and Moira [Moondog Coronation Ball]

Doobie Brothers, The, 3/2013, *Quicken Loans Arena in Cleveland, Ohio,* Terry, Kim and Moira [Moondog Coronation Ball]; 6/2016, *Blossom Music Center in Cuyahoga Falls, Ohio,* Terry and Moira

Double Trouble, 4/2015, *Public Hall in Cleveland, Ohio,* Terry and Moira [Rock and Roll Hall of Fame Ceremony]

Dove Brothers, The, 3/2011, *Westfall High School in Williamsport, Ohio,* Moira, Nan and Pa [Westfall Gospel Sing]

Down East Boys, The, 9/2013, *KFEC Expo Center in Louisville, Kentucky,* Moira, Nan and Pa [National Quartet Convention]

Dupuis, Jay, 8/2013, *St. George Theatre in Memphis, Tennessee,* Terry and Moira [International Elvis Tribute Competition]; 8/2013, *St. George Theatre,* Terry and Moira [International Elvis Tribute Competition final]

Duttons, The, 4/2012, *Packard Music Hall in Warren, Ohio,* Terry, Kim and Moira

Eagles, The, 7/2013, *Quicken Loans Arena in Cleveland, Ohio,* Terry, Kim and Rob Hollada [Moira was making an album ☺]

Easter, Sheri, 4/2012, *Packard Music Hall in Warren, Ohio,* Moira, Nan and Pa; 9/2013 (**Easter, Sheri and Jeff**), *KFEC Expo Center in Louisville, Kentucky,* Moira, Nan and Pa [National Quartet Convention]

Eberline, Maria, 4/2015, *Packard Music Hall in Warren, Ohio,* Terry, Kim and Moira [Neil Berg's 100 Years of Broadway]

Eder, Linda, 11/2013, *Packard Music Hall in Warren, Ohio,* Terry, Kim and Moira [Warren Civic Music program]

Edwards, Donny [Elvis Tribute artist at annual Elvis Birthday Tribute], 1/2011, *Playhouse Square in Cleveland, Ohio,* Terry, Kim and Moira; 1/2012, *Playhouse Square,* Terry, Kim and Moira; 1/2013, *Playhouse Square,* Terry, Kim and Moira; 1/2014, *Playhouse Square,* Terry and Moira; 1/2015, *Playhouse Square,* Terry and Moira

Eleventh Hour, 9/2013, *KFEC Expo Center in Louisville, Kentucky,* Moira, Nan and Pa [National Quartet Convention]

Elvis, Gordon, 8/2013, *St. George Theatre in Memphis, Tennessee,* Terry and Moira [International Elvis Tribute Competition]

Ely, Rob, 8/2013, *St. George Theatre in Memphis, Tennessee,* Terry and Moira [International Elvis Tribute Competition]

Fabulous Ambassadors Band, The, 1/2011, *Playhouse Square in Cleveland, Ohio,* Terry, Kim and Moira; 1/2012, *Playhouse Square,* Terry, Kim and Moira; 1/2013, *Playhouse Square,* Terry, Kim and Moira; 1/2014, *Playhouse Square,* Terry and Moira; 1/2015, *Playhouse Square,* Terry and Moira; 1/2016, *Playhouse Square,* Terry and Moira; 1/2017, *Playhouse Square,* Terry and Moira; 1/2018, *Playhouse Square,* Terry and Moira

Fall Out Boy, 4/2015, *Public Hall in Cleveland, Ohio,* Terry and Moira [Rock and Roll Hall of Fame Ceremony]

Family Stone, The, 3/2014, *Quicken Loans Arena in Cleveland, Ohio,* Terry, Kim and Moira [Moondog Coronation Ball]

Fitzpatrick, Adam, 8/2013, *St. George Theatre in Memphis, Tennessee,* Terry and Moira [International Elvis Tribute Competition]; 8/2013, *St. George Theatre,* Terry and Moira [International Elvis Tribute Competition final]

Five Royales, The, 4/2015, *Public Hall in Cleveland, Ohio,* Terry and Moira [Rock and Roll Hall of Fame Ceremony]

Fleetwood Mac, 2/2015, *Quicken Loans Arena in Cleveland, Ohio,* Terry, Kim and Moira

Fogerty, John, 7/2015, *Jacob's Pavilion in Cleveland, Ohio,* Terry and Moira

Foghat, 7/2014, *Ohio State Fairgrounds-Celeste Center in Columbus, Ohio,* Terry and Moira

Fontana, DJ [Drummer for Elvis Presley], 1/2011, *Playhouse Square in Cleveland, Ohio,* Terry, Kim and Moira; 1/2012, *Playhouse Square,* Terry, Kim and Moira; 1/2013, *Playhouse Square,* Terry, Kim and Moira; 1/2014, *Playhouse Square,* Terry and Moira; 1/2015, *Playhouse Square,* Terry and Moira; 1/2016, *Playhouse Square,* Terry and Moira; 1/2017, *Playhouse Square,* Terry and Moira

Foreigner, 7/2017, *Giant Center in Hershey, PA,* Terry and Moira

Frampton, Peter, 8/2015, *Ohio State Fairgrounds Celeste Center in Columbus, Ohio,* Terry and Moira

Frankie Valli and the Four Seasons, 12/2011, *Playhouse Square in Cleveland, Ohio,* Terry, Kim and Moira

Franklin, Aretha, 7/2014, *Ohio State Fairgrounds-Celeste Center in Columbus, Ohio,* Terry, Kim and Moira

Gaither Vocal Band, 9/2011, *Covelli Center in Youngstown, Ohio,* Moira, Nan and Pa [Gaither Homecoming Tour]; 9/2013, *KFEC Expo Center in Louisville, Kentucky,* Moira, Nan and Pa [National Quartet Convention]

Gaither, Bill and Friends, 9/2012, *KFEC Expo Center in Louisville, Kentucky,* Moira, Nan and Pa [National Quartet Convention]

Galloways, The, 3/2011, *Westfall High School in Williamsport, Ohio,* Moira, Nan and Pa [Westfall Gospel Sing]; 3/2012, *Westfall High School,* Moira, Nan and Pa [Westfall Gospel Sing]; 3/2013, *Westfall High School,* Moira, Nan and Pa [Westfall Gospel Sing]

Geils, j. Band, 12/2014, *Quicken Loans Arena in Cleveland, Ohio,* Terry, Kim and Moira

Generation of Faith, 3/2011, *Westfall High School in Williamsport, Ohio,* Moira, Nan and Pa [Westfall Gospel Sing]; 3/2012, *Westfall High School,* Moira, Nan and Pa [Westfall Gospel Sing]; 3/2013, *Westfall High School,* Moira, Nan and Pa [Westfall Gospel Sing]

Glass Harp, 5/2016, *The Kent Stage in Kent, Ohio,* Terry and Moira

Gold City, 5/2014, *Packard Music Hall,* Moira, Nan, and Pa; 9/2012, *KFEC Expo Center in Louisville, Kentucky,* Moira, Nan and Pa [National Quartet Convention]; 9/2013, *KFEC Expo Center,* Moira, Nan and Pa [National Quartet Convention]

Gordon Mote, 9/2011, *Covelli Center in Youngstown, Ohio,* Moira, Nan and Pa [Gaither Homecoming Tour]

Gore, Tony and Majesty, 3/2013, *Westfall High School in Williamsport, Ohio,* Moira, Nan and Pa [Westfall Gospel Sing]

Grand Ole Opry, 7/2013, *Nashville, Tennesee,* Moira, Nan and Pa, Stamps Baxter Gospel Music School

Grass Roots, The, 9/2015, *Canfield Fairgrounds in Canfield, Ohio,* Terry, Moira and Brittany , Happy Together Tour

Greater Vision, 9/2012, *KFEC Expo Center in Louisville, Kentucky,* Moira, Nan and Pa [National Quartet Convention]; 9/2013, *KFEC Expo Center,* Moira, Nan and Pa [National Quartet Convention]

Green Day, 4/2015, *Public Hall in Cleveland, Ohio,* Terry and Moira [Rock and Roll Hall of Fame Ceremony]

Greene, TaRanda, 3/2013, *Westfall High School in Williamsport, Ohio,* Moira, Nan and Pa [Westfall Gospel Sing]

Grey, Joel, 10/2015, *Playhouse Square in Cleveland, Ohio,* Terry and Moira

Grohl, Dave, 4/2015, *Public Hall in Cleveland, Ohio,* Terry and Moira [Rock and Roll Hall of Fame Ceremony]

Haase, Ernie and Signature Sound, 9/2012, *KFEC Expo Center in Louisville, Kentucky,* Moira, Nan and Pa [National Quartet Convention]

Hall and Oates, 5/2014, *Public Hall in Cleveland, Ohio,* Terry, Kim and Moira

Heart, 7/2014, *Ohio State Fairgrounds-Celeste Center in Columbus, Ohio,* Terry, Kim and Moira; 7/2016, *Riverbend Music Center in Cincinnati, Ohio,* Terry and Moira

Hendry, Tim, 8/2013, *St. George Theatre in Memphis, Tennessee,* Terry and Moira [International Elvis Tribute Competition]

Hoppers, The, 9/2012, *KFEC Expo Center in Louisville, Kentucky,* Moira, Nan and Pa [National Quartet Convention]; 9/2013, *KFEC Expo Center,* Moira, Nan and Pa [National Quartet Convention]

Icenhower, Dwight, 8/2013, *St. George Theatre in Memphis, Tennessee,* Terry and Moira [International Elvis Tribute Competition]

Idol, Billy, 8/2019, *DTE Energy Center in Clarkston, Michigan,* Terry and Moira

Iris, Donnie and the Cruisers, 5/2006, *Boardman Park in Boardman, Ohio,* Terry, Kim, Rob & Sue Holllada; 5/2016, *Warren Community Amphitheater in Warren, Ohio,* Terry and Moira [River Rock at the Amp Series]; 12/2017, *Hard Rockscino in Northfield, Ohio,* Terry, Mark Garramone and Rob Hollada

Isaacs, The, 9/2011, *Covelli Center in Youngstown, Ohio,* Moira, Nan and Pa [Gaither Homecoming Tour]; 9/2013, *KFEC Expo Center in Louisville, Kentucky,* Moira, Nan and Pa [National Quartet Convention]

Isley Brothers, The, 10/2019, *Playhouse Square in Cleveland, Ohio,* Terry, Moira, Jordan and Kit

James, Tommy, 4/2015, *Public Hall in Cleveland, Ohio,* Terry and Moira [Rock and Roll Hall of Fame Ceremony]; 3/2014 **(Tommy James and the Shaundells),** *Quicken Loans Arena in Cleveland, Ohio,* Terry, Kim and Moira [Moondog Coronation Ball]

Jazz Aces with Toni Elizabeth Prima, 11/2012, *Packard Music Hall in Warren, Ohio,* Terry, Kim and Moira

Jeffrey, Terry Mike, 8/2013, *Memphis Tennessee,* Terry and Moira [Part of Elvis Week]

Jett, Joan and the Blackhearts, 6/2013, *Art Park in Buffalo, New York,* Terry and Moira; 7/2014, *Ohio State Fairgrounds-Celeste Center in Columbus, Ohio,* Terry, Kim and Moira; 4/2015, *Public Hall in Cleveland, Ohio,* Terry and Moira [Rock and Roll Hall of Fame Ceremony]; 5/2015, *Nationwide Arena in Columbus, Ohio,* Terry and Moira; 7/2016, *Riverbend Music Center in Cincinnati, Ohio,* Terry and Moira; 6/2018, *Blue Hills Bank Pavilion in Boston, Massachusetts,* Terry and Moira; 7/2019, *Progressive Field in Cleveland, Ohio,* Terry and Moira [Baseball All Star Game Event]

Jim Brickman, 11/2010, *Kent State University-Tuscarawas Art Center,* Terry, Kim and Moira

Joel, Billy, 2/2014, *Consol Energy Center in Pittsburgh, PA,* Terry and Moira; 1/2020, *Madison Square Garden in New York City,* Terry and Moira

John, Elton, 4/2013, *Nutter Center in Dayton, Ohio,* Terry and Moira; 3/2016, *Covelli Center in Youngstown, Ohio,* Terry, Kim and Moira

Journey, 8/2013, *Illinois State Fair in Springfield, Illinois,* Terry and Moira [Illinois State Fair Concert Series]; 6/2016, *Blossom Music Center in Cuyahoga Falls, Ohio,* Terry and Moira

Kansas, 8/2012, *Ohio State Fairgrounds Celeste Center in Columbus, Ohio,* Terry and Moira; 5/2015, *Hard Rockscino in Northfield, Ohio,* Terry and Mark Garramone

Karen Culliver, 9/2011, *Packard Music Hall in Warren, Ohio,* Moira, Nan and Pa [Phantom Leading Ladies]

KC and the Sunshine Band, 4/2012, *Quicken Loans Arena in Cleveland, Ohio,* Terry and Moira [Moondog Coronation Ball]

Keelings, The, 4/2012, *Packard Music Hall in Warren, Ohio,* Moira, Nan and Pa

Kevin Mills, 2/2012, *Lima Civic Center in Lima, Ohio,* Terry and Moira [One of Elvis Tribute Artists (Elvis Lives)]

Kingdom Heirs, The, 9/2012, *KFEC Expo Center in Louisville, Kentucky,* Moira, Nan and Pa [National Quartet Convention]; 9/2013, *KFEC Expo Center,* Moira, Nan and Pa [National Quartet Convention]

Kingsmen, The, 3/2011, *Westfall High School in Williamsport, Ohio,* Moira, Nan and Pa [Westfall Gospel Sing]; 3/2012, *Westfall High School,* Moira, Nan and Pa [Westfall Gospel Sing]; 9/2012, *KFEC Expo Center in Louisville, Kentucky,* Moira, Nan and Pa [National Quartet Convention]; 3/2013, *Westfall High School,* Moira, Nan and Pa [Westfall Gospel Sing]

Kioci, Sato, 8/2013, *St. George Theatre in Memphis, Tennessee,* Terry and Moira [International Elvis Tribute Competition]

Kiss, 8/2014, *Blossom Music Center in Cuyahoga Falls, Ohio,* Terry and Moira; 3/2019, *Quicken Loans Arena in Cleveland, Ohio,* Terry

Klush, Shawn [Elvis Tribute artist at annual Elvis Birthday Tribute], 1/2011, *Playhouse Square in Cleveland, Ohio,* Terry, Kim and Moira; 1/2012, *Playhouse Square,* Terry, Kim and Moira; 1/2013, *Playhouse Square,*

Terry, Kim and Moira; 1/2014, *Playhouse Square,* Terry and Moira; 1/2015, *Playhouse Square,* Terry and Moira; 1/2016, *Playhouse Square,* Terry and Moira; 1/2017, *Playhouse Square,* Terry and Moira; 1/2018, *Playhouse Square,* Terry and Moira

Lady Lamb, 9/2015, *House of Blues in Cleveland, Ohio,* Terry and Moira

Lakewood Project, 3/2015, *Playhouse Square in Cleveland, Ohio,* Terry and Moira [Part of kick off Playhouse Square series]

Lauper, Cyndi, 11/2013, *Quicken Loans Arena in Cleveland, Ohio,* Terry, Kim and Moira [Scott Hamilton Ice Skating benefit show]; 5/2014, *Quicken Loans Arena,* Terry, Kim and Moira

Le Flavour, 5/2012, *Packard Music Hall in Warren, Ohio,* Moira, Nan and Pa

Lee, David, 8/2013, *St. George Theatre in Memphis, Tennessee,* Terry and Moira [International Elvis Tribute Competition]

LeFevre, Mike, 7/2013, *Nashville, Tennessee,* Moira, Nan and Pa [Stamps Baxter Gospel Music School]

Legacy Five, 9/2012, *KFEC Expo Center in Louisville, Kentucky,* Moira, Nan and Pa [National Quartet Convention]; 9/2013, *KFEC Expo Center,* Moira, Nan and Pa [National Quartet Convention]

Legend, John, 4/2015, *Public Hall in Cleveland, Ohio,* Terry and Moira [Rock and Roll Hall of Fame Ceremony]

Letterman, The, 3/2014, *Packard Music Hall in Warren, Ohio,* Moira, Nan and Pa

Lewis, Huey and the News, 7/2015, *Packard Music Hall in Warren, Ohio,* Terry, Kim and Moira

Lewis, Jeff, 8/2013, *St. George Theatre in Memphis, Tennessee,* Terry and Moira [International Elvis Tribute Competition]

Lichwiess, Di, 8/2013, *St. George Theatre in Memphis, Tennessee,* Terry and Moira [International Elvis Tribute Competition]; 8/2013, *St. George Theatre,* Terry and Moira [International Elvis Tribute Competition final]

Lindsey, Mark of Paul Revere and the Raiders, 3/2015, *Quicken Loans Arena in Cleveland, Ohio,* Terry, Moira and Antiggonie [Moondog Coronation Ball]; 9/2015, *Canfield Fairgrounds in Canfield, Ohio,* Terry, Moira and Brittany [Happy Together Tour]

Living Color, 8/2015, *Tom Benson Stadium at the Football Hall of Fame in Canton, Ohio,* Terry and Moira [Football Hall of Fame Ceremony Festival]

Loggins, Kenny, 6/1985, *Blossom Music Center in Cuyahoga Falls, Ohio,* Terry and Frank; 8/2017, *Lorain County Fair in Lorain, Ohio,* Terry, Moira and Mason

Lovelace, Tim, 9/2012, *KFEC Expo Center in Louisville, Kentucky,* Moira, Nan and Pa [National Quartet Convention]; 9/2013, *KFEC Expo Center,* Moira, Nan and Pa [National Quartet Convention]

Lowe Family, The, 12/2013, *Packard Music Hall in Warren, Ohio,* Terry, Kim and Moira

Lulich, Silas, 8/2013, *St. George Theatre in Memphis, Tennessee,* Terry and Moira [International Elvis Tribute Competition]

Luthaker, Steve of Toto, 6/2016, *Riverbend Music Center in Cincinnati, Ohio,* Terry, Moira and Morgan [Ringo Starr All Star Band]

Lynryd Skynyrd, 9/2015, *Fulton County Fair in Wauseon, Ohio,* Terry and Moira

Manilow, Barry, 3/2015, *Wolstein Center in Cleveland Ohio on the campus of Cleveland State University,* Terry, Kim and Moira

Mannheim Steamroller, 11/2009, *Quicken Loans Arena in Cleveland, Ohio,* Terry, Kim and Moira

Marcy D'Arcy, 9/2011, *Packard Music Hall in Warren, Ohio,* Moira, Nan and Pa [Phantom Leading Ladies]

Mark Lowry, 9/2011, *Covelli Center in Youngstown, Ohio,* Moira, Nan and Pa [Gaither Homecoming Tour]

Martins, The, 9/2011, *Covelli Center in Youngstown, Ohio,* Moira, Nan and Pa [Gaither Homecoming Tour]

Marvelettes, The (no original members), 9/2012, *Packard Music Hall in Warren, Ohio,* Terry, Kim and Moira

Mayer, John, 4/2015, *Public Hall in Cleveland, Ohio,* Terry and Moira [Rock and Roll Hall of Fame Ceremony]

McCartney, Paul, 4/2015, *Public Hall in Cleveland, Ohio,* Terry and Moira [Rock and Roll Hall of Fame Ceremony]; 8/2016, *Quicken Loans Arena in Cleveland, Ohio,* Terry, Moira and Dante

McDonald, Gene, 7/2013, *Nashville, Tennesee,* Moira, Nan and Pa [Stamps Baxter Gospel Music School]

McGlamery, Devin, 7/2013, *Nashville, Tennesee,* Moira, Nan and Pa [Stamps Baxter Gospel Music School]

McKameys, The, 3/2011, *Westfall High School in Williamsport, Ohio,* Moira, Nan and Pa [Westfall Gospel Sing]; 3/2012, *Westfall High School,* Moira, Nan and Pa [Westfall Gospel Sing]

Mellencamp, John, 1/2015, *Playhouse Square in Cleveland, Ohio,* Terry, Kim and Moira

Michael English, 9/2011, *Covelli Center in Youngstown, Ohio,* Moira, Nan and Pa [Gaither Homecoming Tour]

Minnick, Johnny, 7/2013, *Nashville, Tennesee,* Moira, Nan and Pa [Stamps Baxter Gospel Music School]

Moore, Sam (of Sam and Dave), 4/2012, *Quicken Loans Arena in Cleveland, Ohio,* Terry and Moira [Moondog Coronation Ball]

Morello, Tom, 4/2015, *Public Hall in Cleveland, Ohio,* Terry and Moira [Rock and Roll Hall of Fame Ceremony]

Mote, Gordon, 9/2013, *KFEC Expo Center in Louisville, Kentucky,* Moira, Nan and Pa [National Quartet Convention]

Mott the Hoople, 4/2019, *Masonic Lodge in Cleveland, Ohio,* Terry and Mike Chaffee

Nelons, The, 9/2013, *KFEC Expo Center in Louisville, Kentucky,* Moira, Nan and Pa [National Quartet Convention]

Newman, Randy, 7/2015, *Heinz Hall in Pittsburgh, PA,* Terry and Moira

Night Ranger, 8/2013, *Illinois State Fair in Springfield, Illinois,* Terry and Moira [Illinois State Fair Concert Series]

Noone, Peter (Herman's Hermits), 3/2014, *Quicken Loans Arena in Cleveland, Ohio,* Terry, Kim and Moira [Moondog Coronation Ball]

O'Jays, 10/2019, *Playhouse Square in Cleveland Ohio,* Terry, Moira, Jordan and Kit

Old Paths, 7/2013, *Nashville, Tennessee,* Moira, Nan and Pa [Stamps Baxter Gospel Music School]

Page, Richard of Mr. Mister, 6/2016, *Riverbend Music Center in Cincinnati, Ohio,* Terry, Moira and Morgan [Ringo Starr All Star Band]

Parker, Ivan, 9/2012, *KFEC Expo Center in Louisville, Kentucky,* Moira, Nan and Pa [National Quartet Convention]

Parton, Dolly, 8/2016, *Ohio State Fairgrounds Celeste Center in Columbus, Ohio,* Terry and Kim

Peck, Karen and New River, 3/2012, *Westfall High School in Williamsport, Ohio,* Moira, Nan and Pa [Westfall Gospel Sing]; 9/2012, *KFEC Expo Center in Louisville, Kentucky,* Moira, Nan and Pa [National Quartet Convention]; 3/2013, *Westfall High School,* Moira, Nan and Pa [Westfall Gospel Sing]; 9/2013, *KFEC Expo Center,* Moira, Nan and Pa [National Quartet Convention]

Pelton, Ryan [Elvis Tribute artist at annual Elvis Birthday Tribute], 1/2016, *Playhouse Square in Cleveland, Ohio,* Terry and Moira; 1/2017, *Playhouse Square,* Terry and Moira; 1/2018, *Playhouse Square,* Terry and Moira

Penny Loafers, The, 9/2013, *KFEC Expo Center in Louisville, Kentucky,* Moira, Nan and Pa [National Quartet Convention]

Perry, Libbi, 7/2013, *Nashville, Tennesee,* Moira, Nan and Pa [Stamps Baxter Gospel Music School]

Perrys, The, 3/2011, *Westfall High School in Williamsport, Ohio,* Moira, Nan and Pa [Westfall Gospel Sing]; 3/2012, *Westfall High School,* Moira, Nan and Pa [Westfall Gospel Sing]; 9/2012, *KFEC Expo Center in Louisville, Kentucky,* Moira, Nan and Pa [National Quartet Convention]; 9/2013, *KFEC Expo Center,* Moira, Nan and Pa [National Quartet Convention]

Pfiefers, The, 9/2012, *KFEC Expo Center in Louisville, Kentucky,* Moira, Nan and Pa [National Quartet Convention]

Phillips, Ernie and the Land of the Sky Boys, 3/2013, *Westfall High School in Williamsport, Ohio,* Moira, Nan and Pa [Westfall Gospel Sing]

Pitcher, Rebecca, 4/2015, *Packard Music Hall in Warren, Ohio,* Terry, Kim and Moira [Neil Berg's 100 Years of Broadway]

Platters Tribute Band, The, 9/2012, *Packard Music Hall in Warren, Ohio,* Terry, Kim and Moira

Powell, Travis, 8/2013, *St. George Theatre in Memphis, Tennessee,* Terry and Moira [International Elvis Tribute Competition]

Primitive Quartet, 9/2012, *KFEC Expo Center in Louisville, Kentucky,* Moira, Nan and Pa [National Quartet Convention]

Primitives, The, 9/2013, *KFEC Expo Center in Louisville, Kentucky,* Moira, Nan and Pa [National Quartet Convention]

Queen (with Adam Lambert), 7/2019, *PPG Paints Arena in Pittsburgh, PA,* Terry and Moira

ReCreation, 5/2013, *United Methodist Church in Howland, Ohio,* Terry, Kim and Moira; 12/2013, *United Methodist Church,* Terry, Kim and Moira

REO Speedwagon, 6/2013, *Ohio State Fairgrounds Celeste Center in Columbus, Ohio,* Terry and Moira

Richie, Lionel, 8/2016, *Covelli Center in Youngstown, Ohio,* Terry, Kim and Moira

Robinson, Smokey, 3/2015, *Quicken Loans Arena in Cleveland, Ohio,* Terry, Moira and Antiggonie [Moondog Coronation Ball]

Rogers, Kenny, 12/2013, *Packard Music Hall in Warren, Ohio,* Terry, Kim and Moira

Rolie, Gregg of Santana and Journey, 6/2016, *Riverbend Music Center in*

Cincinnati, Ohio, Terry, Moira and Morgan [Ringo Starr All Star Band]

Rolling Stones, The, 6/2015, *Heinz Field in Pittsburgh, PA,* Terry and Moira

Roman, Brian, 10/2013, *Packard Music Hall in Warren, Ohio,* Terry, Kim and Moira [Warren Civic Music program]

Royalaires, The, 3/2011, *Westfall High School in Williamsport, Ohio,* Moira, Nan and Pa [Westfall Gospel Sing]; 3/2012, *Westfall High School,* Moira, Nan and Pa [Westfall Gospel Sing]; 3/2013, *Westfall High School,* Moira, Nan and Pa [Westfall Gospel Sing]

Runaway Saints, 7/2015, *Huntington Convention Center in Toledo, Ohio,* Terry, Kim and Moira

Rundgren, Todd, 6/2016, *Riverbend Music Center in Cincinnati, Ohio,* Terry, Moira and Morgan [Ringo Starr All Star Band]

Seeger, Bob and the Silver Bullet Band, 12/2014, *Quicken Loans Arena in Cleveland, Ohio,* Terry, Kim and Moira

Setzer, Brian, 6/2015, *Rose Music Center in Huber Heights, Ohio,* Terry and Moira

Shore, Anthony, 8/2013, *St. George Theatre in Memphis, Tennessee,* Terry and Moira [International Elvis Tribute Competition]

Six, 4/2013, *Packard Music Hall in Warren, Ohio,* Terry, Kim and Moira [Warren Civic Music program]

Slaughter, Cody [Elvis tribute artist at annual Elvis Birthday Tribute], 1/2011, *Playhouse Square in Cleveland, Ohio,* Terry, Kim and Moira; 1/2012, *Playhouse Square,* Terry, Kim and Moira; 1/2013, *Playhouse Square,* Terry, Kim and Moira; 1/2014, *Playhouse Square,* Terry and Moira; 1/2015, *Playhouse Square,* Terry and Moira; 1/2016, *Playhouse Square,* Terry and Moira; 1/2017, *Playhouse Square,* Terry and Moira; 1/2018, *Playhouse Square,* Terry and Moira

Smith, Patti, 4/2015, *Public Hall in Cleveland, Ohio,* Terry and Moira [Rock and Roll Hall of Fame Ceremony]

Soul'd out, 3/2013, *Westfall High School in Williamsport, Ohio,* Moira, Nan and Pa [Westfall Gospel Sing]

Southside Johnny and the Asbury Jukes, 8/2013, *Warren Community Amphitheater in Warren, Ohio,* Terry and Moira [River Rock at the Amph]; 11/2019, *Hard Rock Café in New York City,* Terry and Moira, Rock and Roll Forever Foundation Gala

Speck, Mike, 9/2012, *KFEC Expo Center in Louisville, Kentucky,* Moira, Nan and Pa [National Quartet Convention]

Speer, Allison, 7/2013, *Nashville, Tennessee,* Moira, Nan and Pa, Stamps Baxter Gospel Music School

Speer, Ben, 7/2013, *Nashville, Tennessee,* Moira, Nan and Pa, Stamps Baxter Gospel Music School

Speer, Rosa Neil, 7/2013, *Nashville, Tennesee,* Moira, Nan and Pa, Stamps Baxter Gospel Music School

Springsteen, Bruce and the E Street Band, 4/2012, *Quicken Loans Arena in Cleveland, Ohio,* Terry and Rob Hollada; 11/2012, *Bryce Jordan Center in State College, Pennsylvania (home of Penn State),* Terry and Moira; 2/2016, *Quicken Loans Arena,* Terry and Moira; 9/2016, *Consol Energy Center in Pittsburgh, PA,* Terry and Moira

Stamps, The, 8/2013, *Memphis Tennessee,* Terry and Moira [Part of Elvis Week]

Stanley, Michael and the Resonators, 10/2013, *Packard Music Hall in Warren, Ohio,* Moira, Nan and Pa; 12/2017, *Hard Rockscino in Northfield, Ohio,* Terry, Mark Garramone and Rob Hollada

Starr, Ringo, 4/2015, *Public Hall in Cleveland, Ohio,* Terry and Moira [Rock and Roll Hall of Fame Ceremony]; 10/2015 (**Ringo Starr and his All Starr Band**), 10/2015, *Heinz Hall in Pittsburgh, PA,* Terry and Moira; 6/2016 (**Ringo Starr**

and his All Starr Band), *Riverbend Music Center in Cincinnati, Ohio,* Terry, Moira and Morgan

Steely Dan, 7/2015, *Blossom Music Center in Cuyahoga Falls, Ohio,* Terry and Moira

Steppenwolf, 3/2014, *Quicken Loans Arena in Cleveland, Ohio,* Terry, Kim and Moira [Moondog Coronation Ball]

Steve Miller Band, 7/2013, *Ohio State Fairgrounds Celeste Center in Columbus, Ohio,* Terry and Moira

Stevens, The, 4/2012, *Packard Music Hall in Warren, Ohio,* Moira, Nan and Pa

Stewart, Rod, 7/2015, *Huntington Convention Center in Toledo, Ohio,* Terry, Kim and Moira

Straight No Chaser, 11/2011, *Playhouse Square in Cleveland, Ohio,* Terry, Kim and Moira

Styx, 7/2013, *Ohio State Fairgrounds Celeste Center in Columbus, Ohio,* Terry and Moira; 5/2017, *Stambaugh Auditorium in Youngstown, Ohio,* Terry and Kim; 6/2018, *Blue Hills Bank Pavilion in Boston, Massachusetts,* Terry and Moira

Swanberg, Dennis, 9/2012, *KFEC Expo Center in Louisville, Kentucky,* Moira, Nan and Pa [National Quartet Convention]; 9/2013, *KFEC Expo Center in Louisville, Kentucky,* Moira, Nan and Pa [National Quartet Convention]

Sweet Inspirations [Back up singers for Elvis Presley], 1/2011, *Playhouse Square in Cleveland, Ohio,* Terry, Kim and Moira; 1/2012, *Playhouse Square,* Terry, Kim and Moira; 1/2013, *Playhouse Square,* Terry, Kim and Moira; 1/2014, *Playhouse Square,* Terry and Moira; 1/2015, *Playhouse Square,* Terry and Moira; 1/2016, *Playhouse Square,* Terry and Moira; 1/2017, *Playhouse Square,* Terry and Moira

Tallest Man on Earth, The, 9/2015, *House of Blues in Cleveland, Ohio,* Terry and Moira; 5/2019, *Carnegie of Homestead Music Hall in Pittsburgh, PA,* Terry and Moira

Talleys, The, 9/2012, *KFEC Expo Center in Louisville, Kentucky,* Moira, Nan and Pa [National Quartet Convention]; 9/2013, *KFEC Expo Center,* Moira, Nan and Pa [National Quartet Convention]; 6/2012, *Packard Music Hall in Warren, Ohio,* Moira, Nan and Pa

Taylor, James, 1/2013, *Capitol Building in Washington DC,* Terry and Moira, Presidential Inauguration

Taylors, The, 9/2012, *KFEC Expo Center in Louisville, Kentucky,* Moira, Nan and Pa [National Quartet Convention]; 9/2013, *KFEC Expo Center,* Moira, Nan and Pa [National Quartet Convention]

Temptations, The, 3/2013, *Quicken Loans Arena in Cleveland, Ohio,* Terry, Kim and Moira [Moondog Coronation Ball]

Teri Bibb, 9/2011, *Packard Music Hall in Warren, Ohio,* Moira, Nan and Pa, Phantom Leading Ladies

Tesla, 6/2018, *Blue Hills Bank Pavilion in Boston, Massachusetts,* Terry and Moira

Texas Tenors, 12/2011, *Packard Music Hall in Warren, Ohio,* Terry, Kim and Moira

Thomas, BJ, 3/2015, *Quicken Loans Arena in Cleveland, Ohio,* Terry, Moira and Antiggonie [Moondog Coronation Ball]

Thompson, Ben, 8/2013, *St. George Theatre in Memphis, Tennessee,* Terry and Moira [International Elvis Tribute Competition]; 8/2013, *St. George Theatre,* Terry and Moira [International Elvis Tribute Competition final]

Thorogood, George and the Destroyers, 6/2015, *Rose Music Center in Huber Heights, Ohio,* Terry and Moira

Three Dog Night, 3/2013, *Quicken Loans Arena in Cleveland, Ohio,* Terry, Kim and Moira [Moondog Coronation Ball]

Three Part Invention, 1/2011, *Akron Public Library Main Branch in Akron, Ohio,* Terry, Kim and Moira

Tony Bennett, 10/2011, *Playhouse Square in Cleveland, Ohio,* Terry, Kim and Moira

Torres, Ted, 8/2013, *St. George Theatre in Memphis, Tennessee,* Terry and Moira [International Elvis Tribute Competition]

Tracey Silverman, 11/2010, *Kent State University-Tuscarawas Art Center,* Terry, Kim and Moira

Trammell, Mark (Quartet), 9/2012, *KFEC Expo Center in Louisville, Kentucky,* Moira, Nan and Pa [National Quartet Convention]; 9/2013, *KFEC Expo Center,* Moira, Nan and Pa [National Quartet Convention]

Tribute Quartet, 9/2012, *KFEC Expo Center in Louisville, Kentucky,* Moira, Nan and Pa [National Quartet Convention]

Triumphant Quartet, 3/2011, *Westfall High School in Williamsport, Ohio,* Moira, Nan and Pa [Westfall Gospel Sing]; 3/2012, *Westfall High School,* Moira, Nan and Pa [Westfall Gospel Sing]; 3/2013, *Westfall High School,* Moira, Nan and Pa [Westfall Gospel Sing]

U2, 6/2017, *Heinz Field in Pittsburgh, PA,* Terry and Moira

Ulisse, Donna and the Poor Mountain Boys, 7/2013, *Nashville, Tennessee,* Moira, Nan and Pa [Stamps Baxter Gospel Music School]

Van Zandt, Stevie (and the Disciples of Soul), 11/2018, *Hard Rockscino in Northfield, Ohio,* Terry and Mark Garramone; 11/2019, *Hard Rock Café in New York City,* Terry and Moira [Rock and Roll Forever Foundation Gala]

Vaughn, Jimmy, 4/2015, *Public Hall in Cleveland, Ohio,* Terry and Moira [Rock and Roll Hall of Fame Ceremony]

Victor Trevino, 2/2012, *Lima Civic Center in Lima, Ohio,* Terry and Moira [One of Elvis Tribute Artists (Elvis Lives)]

Voices of Lee, 9/2012, *KFEC Expo Center in Louisville, Kentucky,* Moira, Nan and Pa [National Quartet Convention]; 9/2013, *KFEC Expo Center,* Moira, Nan and Pa [National Quartet Convention]

Waites, Ben, 7/2013, *Nashville, Tennesee,* Moira, Nan and Pa, Stamps Baxter Gospel Music School

Walsh, Joe, 4/2015, *Public Hall in Cleveland, Ohio,* Terry and Moira [Rock and Roll Hall of Fame Ceremony]; 9/2015, *Packard Music Hall in Warren, Ohio,* Terry and Moira

Warren Philharmonic Orchestra, 10/2010, *Christ Episcopal Church in Warren, Ohio,* Terry, Kim and Moira

Webb, Rick and Family, 9/2013, *KFEC Expo Center in Louisville, Kentucky,* Moira, Nan and Pa [National Quartet Convention]

Whisnants, The, 9/2012, *KFEC Expo Center in Louisville, Kentucky,* Moira, Nan and Pa [National Quartet Convention]; 9/2013, *KFEC Expo Center in Louisville, Kentucky,* Moira, Nan and Pa [National Quartet Convention]

Who, The, 5/2015, *Nationwide Arena in Columbus, Ohio,* Terry and Moira

Wilburn and Wilburn, 3/2011, *Westfall High School in Williamsport, Ohio,* Moira, Nan and Pa [Westfall Gospel Sing]; 3/2012, *Westfall High School,* Moira, Nan and Pa [Westfall Gospel Sing]

Williams, Eli, 8/2013, *St. George Theatre in Memphis, Tennessee,* Terry and Moira [International Elvis Tribute Competition]

Withers, Bill, 4/2015, *Public Hall in Cleveland, Ohio,* Terry and Moira [Rock and Roll Hall of Fame Ceremony]

Wolf, Peter, 4/2015, *Public Hall in Cleveland, Ohio,* Terry and Moira [Rock and Roll Hall of Fame Ceremony]

Wolfe, Gerald, 9/2013, *KFEC Expo Center in Louisville, Kentucky,* Moira, Nan and Pa [National Quartet Convention]

Wolfe, Richard, 8/2013, *St. George Theatre in Memphis, Tennessee,* Terry and Moira [International Elvis Tribute Competition]

Wonder, Stevie, 4/2015, *Public Hall in Cleveland, Ohio,* Terry and Moira [Rock and Roll Hall of Fame Ceremony]

Wright, Cliff, 8/2013, *St. George Theatre in Memphis, Tennessee,* Terry and Moira [International Elvis Tribute Competition]; 8/2013, *St. George Theatre,* Terry and Moira [International Elvis Tribute Competition final]

Zanier, Jay, 8/2013, *St. George Theatre in Memphis, Tennessee,* Terry and Moira [International Elvis Tribute Competition]

Zolli, Danny, 4/2015, *Packard Music Hall in Warren, Ohio,* Terry, Kim and Moira [Neil Berg's 100 Years of Broadway]

ZZ Top, 10/ 2015, *Cambria County War Memorial Arena in Johnstown, PA,* Terry and Moira

X Ambassarors The, 11/2019, *House of Blues in Cleveland, Ohio,* Terry and Moira

Yankovic, Al Weird, 5/2015, *Jacob's Pavilion in Cleveland, Ohio,* Terry and Moira; 6/2016, *Akron Civic Theater in Akron, Ohio,* Terry and Moira; 6/2019, *Playhouse Square in Cleveland,* Terry, Kim and Moira

Yo Yo Ma, 8/2010, *Blossom Music Center in Cuyahoga Falls, Ohio,* Terry, Kim and Moira

MEET THE BAND

About the Authors

A native of the Mahoning Valley in Northeast Ohio, **Terry Armstrong** is a proud husband to Kim and dad to Moira. Following several years in the private sector, he followed his dream of becoming a teacher, earning a Bachelors Degree from Kent State University and Masters Degree from the University of Cincinnati. In addition to being fortunate to have the best students any teacher could ever imagine, Terry was awarded the National Time Warner Teacher of the Year and the *Tribune Chronicle* A+ Teacher Award, and he is a member of the LaBrae High School Hall of Fame. Following his teaching career, he became Superintendent of Lordstown Local Schools and later combined his interest in education with his finance experience as a school treasurer. Terry cherishes his friends and is a fan of Cleveland sports teams, reading, politics, and of course a good concert!

Moira Armstrong, an aspiring professor, is a member of the Honors College at Kent State University majoring in English and History. Moira is the author of two poetry chapbooks, *who lives like this for such a cheap price* (Flower Press) and *the truth about the sky* (Selcouth Station); a reader for *Prismatica Magazine*; and an editor for *Fusion* and *Curtain Call* magazines. Moira's work is published or forthcoming in *Qwerty*, *Brainchild*, and *bed zine*, among others. Find them online @mpawrites and at mpawrites.wixsite.com/website.

Please reach out to us on social media

Moira

Twitter and Instagram @mpawrites

LinkedIn Moira Armstrong (*www.linkedin.com/in/mparmstrong*)

Email mpawrites@gmail.com

Terry

Twitter @rockandrollatoz

LinkedIn Terry Armstrong (*terry-armstrong-2629948*)

Email mistertarmstrong@yahoo.com
(*and don't forget the T in the middle –
Terry pities the fool who does!*)